RAF WATTISHAM
A PICTORIAL HISTORY

RAF WATTISHAM
A PICTORIAL HISTORY

DAVE EADE

FOREWORD BY
AIR MARSHAL SIR ROY AUSTEN-SMITH KBE CB LVO DSC

PUBLICATIONS

CONTENTS

FOREWORD   *Air Marshal Sir Roy Austen-Smith*   KBE CB CVO DFC   7

BIRTH OF AN AIRFIELD   8

PREPARING FOR WAR   10

BEARING THE BRUNT   12

    The Awful Noise of Shells   *Flying Officer Richard Millar, No 110 Squadron*   15

    Searching for the Scharnhorst   *Aircraftman Tom Payne, No 110 Squadron*   16

    The Vital Signals   *Sergeant Colin Beechinor, SHQ Signals*   16

NEW MANAGEMENT   22

    One of the Best Airfields in England   *Corporal Guy Purdy, 434th Fighter Squadron*   24

    Exactly What I Needed   *Colonel 'Dee' Harper, 434th Fighter Squadron*   24

    Mock Combat with the RAF   *Major Robert Munson, 434th Fighter Squadron*   28

POSTWAR PAUSE   32

METEOR MEMORIES   34

    Learning the Hard Way   *Air Commodore 'Mac' McEwen* AFC, *No 257 Squadron*   38

    Commemorating the Greatest Battle   *The Author*   40

HUNTER HEAVEN   46

    Scrambled at Sundown   *Colonel Howard N. Tanner, No 257 Squadron*   48

    Supersonic Ejection   *The Author*   50

'You Can't Come in Yet!' *Air Commodore 'Mac' McEwen* AFC, *No 257 Squadron*   52
The Day My Engine Died   *Squadron Leader Brian Weeden, No 257 Squadron*   53
The 'Black Arrows' Come to Wattisham   *Air Commodore Roger Topp* DFC**, *No 111 (F) Squadron*   56

SEEK AND DESTROY   60

WATCHING EYES   64
The Curve of the 'C'   *Airman First Class Don Lamoreaux*   65
Tinsmith Trouble   *Corporal John Dell*   67

VERTICAL VELOCITY   68
Special Memories   *Air Chief Marshal Sir Michael Graydon* GCB CBE, *No 56 (F) Squadron*   69
Sworn to Secrecy   *Air Commodore 'Mac' McEwen* AFC, *No 56 (F) Squadron*   70
Leading the Firebirds   *Group Captain David Seward, No 56 (F) Squadron*   74

PHANTOM FINALE   80
Sky Flash at Mach 1.6   *Wing Commander Willem Felger, No 23 (F) Squadron*   82
Tiger Trails   *Group Captain Dick Northcote* OBE BA, *No 74 (F) Squadron*   84
'Q'   *Wing Commander Dave Gledhill, No 56 (F) Squadron*   87
The Final Option   *The Author*   88
Number One Hitter   *Group Captain Graham Clarke, No 74 (F) Squadron*   90

HOVERING HEROES   92

NEW TENANTS   94

PREFACE

Having a father and older brother who were members of the Royal Observer Corps, it is probably not too surprising that I grew up with a passion for military aircraft. From the mid-1950s I have travelled from my homes in Suffolk to spend what some would consider wasted hours —nay, days—at and around RAF Wattisham's Crash Gate 2 watching aircraft coming and going.

The idea of putting my memories in writing was, originally, that of Gary Parsons, for inclusion in his *AirScene UK* internet magazine, and I am indebted to him for this opportunity; the further opportunity to produce this written volume was, again, one not to be missed, and my thanks go to Roger Chesneau of Ad Hoc Publications for his enthusiasm and skills in compiling the present work.

A work of this nature relies heavily on the help and involvement of other people, and I would first like to record my indebtedness to Air Marshal Sir Roy Austen-Smith for kindly agreeing to write the Fore-word for the book. I would like to extend my thanks also to Group Captain Tony Alcock, Linn Barringer, Colin Beechinor, Eric Beechinor, Wing Commander Brian Carruthers, Mary Churchill, Group Captain Graham Clarke, Roger Cook, Bob Cossey, Graham Day (Air Historical Branch—RAF), John Dell, Flight Lieu-tenant Bob Dewes, Walt Farley, Wing Commander Willem Felger, Gerry Fielding, Dave Gledhill, Air Chief Marshal Sir Michael Graydon, Joop de Groot, Colonel 'Dee' Harper, Norman Honeybell, Philip Jarrett, William E. Jones of the Hoosier Air Museum, David Keeble, Don Lamoreaux, Roger Lindsay, Air Commodore 'Mac' McEwen, Roger Marchant, Richard Millar, Hedley Molland, Group Captain Dick North-cote, David Octon, Geoff Parselle, Gary Parsons, Guy Purdy, Rob Rooker, Jerry Scutts, Group Captain David Seward, Graham Smith, John Smith, John Stanaway, Gary Stedman, Colonel Howard N. Tanner, Christine Thurston, Air Commodore Roger Topp, David Vernon, Richard L. Ward, Squadron Leader Brian Weeden and Reg Wyness. It is with great sadness, however, that I have to record that three of the former Wattisham servicemen who assisted with the book, Harry Fryer, Robert Munson and Tom Payne, passed away before the results of their efforts could be published. The assistance rendered by the helpful and friendly staff of the Imperial War Museum and of the Wattisham Air-field Museum is also gratefully acknowledged, as is that readily given by The Blenheim Society. Lastly, I thank my family and the friends who have given me support, not only in this venture but throughout my life.

This book is dedicated to the memory of Dave Woods—a true friend.

Dave Eade
Stowmarket, May 2008

RAF Wattisham Station Officers Commanding

RAF Wattisham Station Officers Commanding

Gp Capt O. R. Gayford OBE DFC AFC
(03/04/39)
Wg Cdr N. C. Singer DSO DFC
(30/04/41)
Gp Capt F. J. W. Hellersh AFC
(21/12/41)
Sqn Ldr L. E. Barry (24/08/42)
Col D. R. Greene USAAF (08/05/43)
Col B. A. Molter USAAF (28/05/43)
Col H. A. Moody USAAF (14/12/43)
Col K. L. Riddle USAAF (16/05/44)
Col H. Zemke USAAF (12/08/44)
Col K. L. Riddle USAAF (01/11/44)
Wg Cdr A. H. Boyd DSO DFC
(21/04/46)
Wg Cdr R. C. F. Lister DFC
(07/11/46)
Wg Cdr C. M. M. Crece DFC
(05/09/49)
Gp Capt V. Acheson OBE
(28/11/50)
Gp Capt H. A. V. Hogan (18/06/51)
Gp. Capt P. G. Wykeham-Barnes
DSO DFC OBE AFC (12/05/52)
Gp Capt H. J. Edwards VC DSO OBE DFC
(28/09/53)
Gp Capt R. J. Gosnell DSO DFC
(15/03/56)
Wg Cdr J. E. Watts AFC (02/09/57)
Gp Capt E. J. Morris DSO DFC
(01/05/58)
Gp Capt B. P. T. Horsley MVO AFC
(09/12/59)
Gp Capt D. C. H. Simmons AFC BA
(15/03/62)
Gp Capt C. M. Gibbs CBE DFC
(27/09/63)
Gp Capt H. Neubroch OBE
(05/08/66)
Gp Capt R. D. Austen-Smith DFC
(06/12/68)
Gp Capt J. Mellers DFC (30/01/70)
Gp. Capt K. J. Goodwin AFC
(08/03/72)
Gp Capt H. Davison OBE (08/05/74)
Gp Capt R. D. Stone AFC (28/05/76)
Gp Capt W. B. G. Hopkins AFC
(23/06/78)
Gp Capt P. J. L. Gover AFC BSc
(27/06/80)
Gp Capt A. J. Park (10/12/82)
Gp Capt G. A. Robertson CBE BA
(14/01/85)
Gp Capt M. P. Donaldson MBE
(00/06/87)
Gp Capt F. S. Rance (00/06/89)
Gp Capt A. J. H. Alcock MBE
(20/09/91)
Wg Cdr S. Blackburn (00/11/92)
(OC Admin)

FOREWORD

Air Marshal Sir Roy Austen-Smith KBE CB CVO DFC

LASTING FRIENDSHIPS

I need hardly say that it was a joy and privilege to have commanded Royal Air Force Wattisham when it was operating two squadrons of the Lightning F.3 aircraft—Nos 29 and 111, at that time commanded by Wing Commander Phipps and Wing Commander Swart, respectively. My two main regrets were that my tour, a mere thirteen months, passed all too quickly, and, secondly, that the runway had to be resurfaced during that short time with the squadrons being temporarily moved to Coltishall and Binbrook.

Nevertheless, I will always remember Wattisham for its location, deep in the Suffolk countryside, and for the friendships that I made with so many of those living in the neighbourhood of what, it has to be admitted, could at times be a rather noisy airfield—music to some but not to others.

It was with great reluctance that I handed over command on 30 January 1970, although at the same time I was glad to know that my memories of RAF Wattisham would always be happy ones. As clearly illustrated in this most interesting and informative book, I realise that I must be but one of a host of others who over the years remember their time at Wattisham with very much the same sort of affection.

Should memories have faded, *RAF Wattisham: A Pictorial History* will certainly rekindle them and provide the reader with a fascinating and most informative account of the history of the Station, presented in chronological order from its birth in April 1939 to the present day. Throughout the book the story is brought to life by the inclusion of many personal recollections contributed by those who served on the base, both in the air and on the ground, as well by a colourful and impressive display of photographs of the many different types of fighter aircraft which operated from the airfield for so many years after the departure of the Blenheims.

On Sunday 15 May 2005 a postscript was added to the history of RAF Wattisham, even though by that time the base had become an Army Air Corps station called Wattisham Airfield. On that particular day the RAF Wattisham War Memorial was dedicated in a very moving ceremony to the remembrance of all those who had given their lives in World War II while serving at the Station. The construction of the Memorial, an idea which from the outset had received strong support from the local community, was funded totally by individual contributions from near and far, including a generous donation from the veterans of the 479th Fighter Group USAAF. Others were generous with the provision of labour and materials. It truly was a team effort—and a true reflection of the close relationship that had existed for years between the RAF station and their most friendly of Wattisham neighbours.

Whatever the future may hold for Wattisham Airfield, may this long-standing friendship be cherished and kept alive.

R.D.A.-S.

7

BIRTH OF AN AIRFIELD

RAF Wattisham originated with the realisation by the British Government in the 1930s that, like it or not, things were going to get worse in Europe before they got better. Some may say, with justification, that it was almost criminal that, in the light of the sacrifice paid by our soldiers in the 1914–18 conflict, this country found itself so ill-equipped for a further conflict that would tear Europe apart.

With the massive rise in strength of the Nazi war machine, sense finally prevailed in the mid-1930s and a rapid expansion of British forces began. Factories were put to work to try to bring our separate military commands up to date. Rapidly, land was acquired in the east of the country, amongst this being three farms, including that of Mr W. Hunt, along with a Roman road (the route of which follows the line of the entrance to the base) in the village of Wattisham, near Stowmarket in Suffolk. Under the auspices of J. Laing & Sons, these farms were totally removed in the creation of a light bomber station, equipped with four large C-type hangars and grass runways. Two roads, one from Great Bricett to Ringshall and that from Bricett to Wattisham, were obliterated from the map in the process. Labour was drawn from the surrounding farms and district, and completion took nearly eighteen months. Drainage was a major problem during and after construction, but the layout followed the standard pattern for all the airfields built in this expansion period; even today, many RAF stations have the same 'look' about them. Portions of the Roman road are still in existence.

On completion of the project, Wing Commander O. R. Gayford officially took over the new station on 6 April 1939 and immediately two squadrons of Bristol Blenheims, Nos 107 and 110, took up residence. Ipswich Airport, opened in the late 1930s, became a satellite of Wattisham.

Right: The bodies of many of those stationed at Wattisham who gave their lives, both during the war and afterwards, are laid to rest in local churchyards such as at Ringshall and Hitcham.

Left: A schematic map showing Wattisham and surrounding district in the late nineteenth century. Land over 250 feet above sea level is shaded dark green—and this in large part explains the choice of site by the Air Ministry. Even so, efficient drainage has proved to be a recurring problem at the Station.

Right: Brigadier-General Kyle Riddle USAF Retd, who was the Commanding Officer at Wattisham from 1 November 1944 until the end of the war in Europe when the 479th Fighter group was in residence, lays a wreath on the occasion of the dedication of the war memorial erected in remembrance of all those who gave their lives while serving at the Station. The memorial, which is situated along the public road to the north of the airfield, was unveiled in 2005.

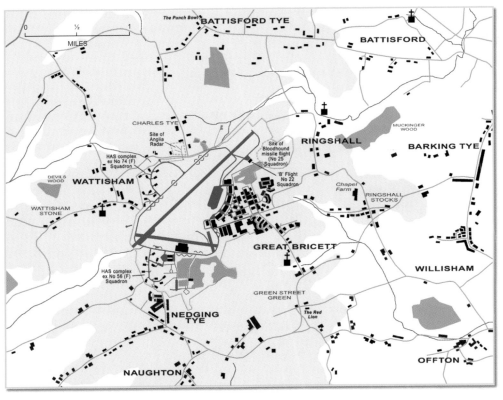

Right: The same area of terrain as that depicted opposite but here as it appeared in the late 1980s, showing the layout of the airfield runways and facilities. Remnants of the road leading past the demolished Honeypot Cottage can still be seen near to the present-day war memorial and part of it survives on the airfield proper, close to the present-day RAF search-and-rescue facility. Remnants of former public thoroughfares can also be seen alongside Ringshall Old Post Office and to the south-west of the airfield, where the old Roman road was truncated when RAF Wattisham was first established.

PREPARING FOR WAR

IF THERE were such things as aircraft spotters in the late 1930s, they would have been going crazy on the morning of 11 May 1939: after nearly two years of construction work, the airfield at Wattisham was ready to receive its aircraft—and the sky that day was full of them.

The first to arrive were the ex-Harwell Blenheim Mk Is of No 107 Squadron, commanded by Squadron Leader Tuttle. It is reported that Blenheim L1279 was the first aircraft to land at Wattisham that day, and by late in the evening all the others were on the ground. At the same time, from Waddington in Lincolnshire, came No 110 Squadron, led by Squadron Leader Cameron with similar Blenheims. The two squadrons formed part of 83 Wing, No 2 Group, and each took up residence in the C-type hangars. By the end of the month, however, both squadrons had converted to the more familiar Blenheim Mk IV with the longer nose.

Life at Wattisham in the early days is related by Christine Thurston of Great Finborough, whose father, Arthur Ashton, was one of the first members of No 110 Squadron to arrive. He was immediately the beneficiary of confusion at the aerodrome as the staff mistook 'Ashton' for 'Adjutant' and treated NCO Arthur with the appropriate respect for such an officer by sending a staff car (complete with flags) to collect him from the railway station!

The arrival of uniformed young men at Wattisham attracted the attention of the similarly aged ladies of the neighbourhood, although not to the level of the later arrivals from across the Atlantic. Favourite ale houses were The Greyhound in Stowmarket and The Punch Bowl in Battisford. Friendships were carved with local farm workers, resulting in the attachment of bomb-trolleys to tractors to provide transport to the local hostelries for refreshment. This was in contrast to the officers, many of whom, on somewhat higher pay scales, could afford to own motor cars and travel further afield, to the outlying villages of Lavenham, Chelsworth and Kersey.

Preparations for war took the form of exercises, and this was to be the routine for the next few months. Tasks included the gathering of fuel consumption and range data and giving anti-aircraft firing practice to our own gunners and, across the Channel, to those of our French allies. Unbeknown to the squadrons, the exercises over France were also providing research data for the new RDF (radio direction-finding, or radar) systems recently installed and now being tested along the south and east coasts of England.

The biggest of all the exercises was that flown during the week 5–11 August. By now war with Germany was considered to be inevitable, and the exercise covered the entirety of the British mainland. Unfortunately, the event was to bring the first taste of tragedy to No 107 Squadron. Having been tasked with putting a nine-aircraft formation up over Dover, the flight moved towards Brighton, ran into inclement weather and turned inland. Finding themselves over the heights of Beachy Head and not, as thought, over low ground, the pilots were forced to climb rapidly, into cloud. Seven of the nine aircraft carried out this manoeuvre

Below: The Prime Minister, Neville Chamberlain, broadcasts over the wireless the news that Britain and Germany are at war, 3 September 1939.

AD HOC COLLECTION

Right: Short-nose Blenheims offer anti-aircraft practice to gunners manning a mobile 40mm Bofors gun during the summer of 1939.

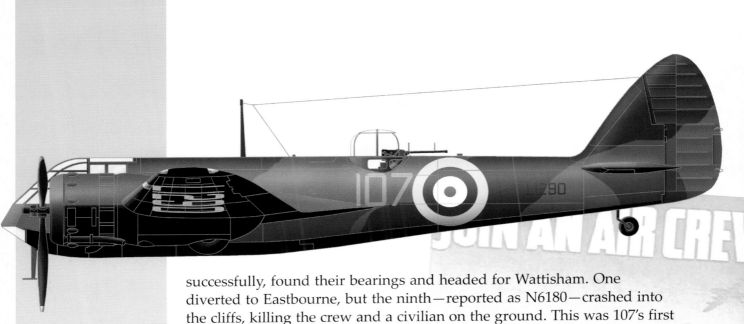

Above: A 'short-nose' Bristol Blenheim Mk I of No 107 Squadron, based at Wattisham shortly after the Station opened. These aircraft were very rapidly replaced by 'long-nose' Blenheim Mk IVs and by the outbreak of war had disappeared from the airfield.

successfully, found their bearings and headed for Wattisham. One diverted to Eastbourne, but the ninth—reported as N6180—crashed into the cliffs, killing the crew and a civilian on the ground. This was 107's first accident since it had re-formed in 1936.

On 24 August the airfield was brought to readiness for war. This included the dispersal of aircraft (on twelve hours' readiness) all round the Station, the bringing in of reservists, the introduction of 'black-outs' and the cancellation of all leave. On the 29th the Station was inspected by Air Chief Marshal Sir Edgar Ludlow-Hewitt, who was then AOC Bomber Command.

When Germany invaded Poland on 1 September 1939 the Station was brought to war status. The two squadrons were assigned to the 2nd Echelon, Advanced Air Striking Force (AASF), roads to and from the airfield were closed, fences were erected at 'strategic' points and gun sites around the Station were manned. No 110 Squadron bolt-holed to Ipswich aerodrome with half of its aircraft. Wattisham was ready for war.

YOUR COURAGE
YOUR CHEERFULNESS
YOUR RESOLUTION
WILL BRING
US VICTORY

BEARING THE BRUNT

O N 4 SEPTEMBER 1939, the day after war was declared, the Royal Air Force launched its first bombing raid when five Blenheims from Wattisham's No 107 Squadron and five from the Ipswich-based No 110 Squadron took off at 1600 hours, their target the German pocket-battleship *Admiral Scheer*. The first bombs to be dropped by any combatant in World War II descended towards the enemy ship, which was hit twice by aircraft of No 110 Squadron.

Only one of No 110's aircraft was lost on this sortie, but nothing was heard again from four of the five Blenheims from No 107 Squadron and only one returned—its weapons still in place. The flight had had difficulty finding the target owing to heavy rain and very low cloud. One aircraft (reported as being N6189) crashed on the deck of the light cruiser *Emden* and two of its crewmen, taken prisoner, gained the unwanted distinction of becoming the first prisoners-of-war of the 1939–45 conflict.

On the aircraft's return, the squadrons, expecting reprisal raids, were detached to Brize Norton for a period, although they were obliged to

No 107 Squadron
Lowestoft's 'own' squadron

Motto
Nous y Serons
('We shall be there')

Equipment
Bristol Blenheim Mk IV light
bombers (code letters 'OM')

Right: The German 'pocket battleship' *Admiral Scheer*, attacked by Wattisham's and Ipswich's Blenheims the day after war was declared.

Below: Preparing one of No 110 Squadron's Blenheim Mk IVs for action.

return to Wattisham for arming and briefing prior to setting off on further raids. This 'logistics chain', together with the high level of unserviceability of the Blenheims, became a concern, and No 107's new Officer Commanding, Wing Commander Basil E. Embry, set about removing the problem. The result was dispersal. However, even aircraft dispersed

IMPERIAL WAR MUSEUM

BRISTOL BLENHEIM Mk IV

Type: Light bomber
Engines: Two 905hp Bristol Mercury XV radials
Length: 42ft 7in (12.98m)
Wing span: 56ft 4in (17.17m)
Speed: 260mph (420kph) maximum
Range: 1,460 miles (2,350km)
Armament: One fixed and two turret-mounted Browning .303 machine guns plus (some aircraft) one or two rearward-firing machine guns in undernose blister; 1,000lb (450kg) bomb load
Crew: Three (pilot, navigator and wireless operator/gunner)

Left: Damage assessment in one of Wattisham's hangars following a raid by a No 110 Squadron Blenheim

No 110 (Hyderabad) Squadron
Ipswich's 'own' squadron, and one of three towards which the Nizam of Hyderabad contributed funds

Motto
Nec Timeo Nec Sperno
('I neither fear nor despise')

Equipment
Bristol Blenheim Mk IV light bombers (code letters 'VE')

around the Station were up to a mile distant from maintenance hangars, and this difficulty, added to that posed by a shortage of transport vehicles, presented new concerns.

The rôle of the two squadrons changed slightly as the number of reconnaissance flights were increased, in order to obtain photographs of suitable targets. These high-value missions earned huge praise but were risky affairs, flown over the Reich in the face of defending Messerschmitt 109s. For example, two No 110 Squadron aircraft, one flown by the CO, took off on such a mission on 27 September 1939 but neither returned.

The latter part of the year became known as the 'Phoney War' due in part to its lack of activity. The severe winter saw heavy snowfalls and further losses when two No 107 Squadron Blenheims failed to return from their missions immediately after Christmas. Deep snow caused the station to be cut off in January 1940, and with the thaw the airfield became a mud-bath. The movement of aircraft—there were no concrete runways or taxiways—became a nightmare both at Wattisham and at the Ipswich dispersal. Some aircraft were transferred to Martlesham Heath, but to little avail. Success did, however, come for No 107 Squadron with the sinking of a U-boat off the German coast. Part of the defence from enemy bombers was in the form of decoy airfields, and during this period two of these were built at Boxford, some eight miles south-west of Wattisham.

By early April 1940 the 'Phoney War' was over and the action intensified. Reconnaissance flights were increased and finally, on the 7th of that

14

The Awful Noise of Shells

Flying Officer Richard Millar, pilot, No 110 Squadron

At the start of the war, No 2 Group had been designated the Advanced Air Striking Force, to work in conjunction with the British Expeditionary Force in France. At this time the Group had three bases in France with squadrons flying Fairey Battles and three in England, Wyton, Watton and Wattisham, each flying two squadrons of Blenheim IVs. Nos 110 and 107 Squadrons were based at Wattisham though in April 1940 detached to Lossiemouth for the Norwegian campaign. Both squadrons were ordered by 2 Group to return to home base as soon as the invasion of the Low Countries was under way.

I was back at Wattisham by 6 May and standing by with my crew—Sergeant Duffy as observer (navigator) and Aircraftsman Greenwood as WOP/AG (wireless operator/air gunner)—from dawn to dusk each day. On 11 May No 110 Squadron was ordered to try to destroy the Maastricht Bridge, giving time to the BEF to get into position and hold back a German advance into France.

No 110 Squadron sent twelve Blenheim IVs in four 'vics' of three led by Flight Lieutenant Gratton, with me flying number three in the rear 'vic'. It was recommended that we fly to the target at 4,000 feet as it was thought that at that altitude we would be too high for the light anti-aircraft guns and too low for the 'heavies' to attack us effectively. How wrong they were! Each Blenheim was loaded with two 250-pound bombs and twelve 40-pound anti-personnel bombs to destroy the bridge and the men crossing it. As ours would be the last Blenheim over the target, our WOP/AG was given a small Leica camera to film the damage done. My crew and I were assigned to P4860.

On 11 May standby started at 0430 and we finally took off to bomb the bridge at 1450. It was a fine, sunny day, with fair-weather cumulus clouds along our route, their bases just over 4,000 feet above the ground. The Squadron flew in a very tight formation so as to present a concentrated defence in case of enemy fighters.

As we neared the target, Sergeant Duffy lay down to operate the bomb sight and called for 'Master switch on.' The navigation by the leading aircraft was spot on: even I at the back could see the bridge in the near distance on our starboard side. Then all hell was let loose as the German anti-aircraft fire got going. Our leader, Flight Lieutenant Gratton, was hit just as he was starting a small turn to line up the formation for the run-in; his aircraft was already burning on the ground as our new leader started to complete the turn for the run-in.

At the final briefing before leaving, it had been impressed on us to keep in close formation when we bombed, to ensure maximum effect. In view of this instruction, and in spite of the awful noise of shells exploding around our aircraft and the black smoke filling the air, I was still keeping close formation on the leader of the rear 'vic' of three. Suddenly all went quiet and his aircraft disappeared from sight as, unknowingly, we went into the base of a fair-weather cloud close to the target area. I can only suppose that I dropped back from him in case of collision, but almost immediately we were out of the cloud again and to my amazement, and that of my crew, there was absolutely no sign of our squadron formation anywhere.

We were now getting close to the bridge, and if we were going to bomb it we had better get on with it. I told Sergeant Duffy over the R/T that I was going down as low as possible and would attack the target diagonally from port to starboard, lengthwise over the bridge, to inflict as much damage as possible with our eleven-second-delay bomb load, and as we came out of the cloud we were in just the right position to carry this action out. Fortunately the enemy AA fire had, if anything, lessened at this point.

We were lucky. We bombed the bridge and got clear without further trouble, and I flew away from the bridge as close to the ground as I dared. There seemed nothing else to now do but make for our home base, keeping a sharp look-out for any other members of the formation. Sergeant Duffy's navigation was extremely good, and when we got to the French coast I gained height as we flew over the Channel for our return to Wattisham, where we landed at 1754.

Below right: The crew of a Blenheim IV of No 2 Group and their ground personnel prepare for a sortie.

month, a large raid was mounted on the enemy fleet, which included the battlecruisers *Scharnhorst* and *Gneisenau*. Although all bombs were dropped, no hits were recorded and the Blenheims, many damaged, headed for home. Almost immediately the two squadrons were removed to Lossiemouth in Scotland as a response to the invasion by the Nazis of Denmark and Norway.

Left: Profile of a Blenheim Mk IV assigned to No 110 Squadron at Wattisham in the standard day bomber scheme of the early months of the war—Dark Earth and Dark Green uppersurfaces and Sky Type 'S' undersurfaces. All unit insignia and other obvious identification markings had been removed from front-line aircraft by the outbreak of war, replaced by a two-letter code denoting the squadron and a single letter identifying the individual aircraft within that squadron.

AD HOC COLLECTION

Searching for the Scharnhorst

Aircraftman Tom Payne, WOp/AG, No 110 Squadron

I arrived at Wattisham in November 1941 from No 13 Squadron at Odiham, feeling rather lonely as my pilot, Pilot Officer Topley, and navigator had caught an earlier train and gone straight to the Officers' Mess. Going into the Sergeants' Mess, I felt that nobody noticed me! My crew had come to help No 110 Squadron re-form after being in Malta. On our second day we were introduced to Wing Commander Cree, the Squadron CO, and allocated to 'A' Flight under Squadron Leader Walters. We flew on each of the first three days, to acclimatise ourselves with the surrounding countryside.

We had to catch a lorry to take us to our dispersal, carrying our two Browning guns with us. Mounting the guns in the turret was not an easy task if there happened to be an easterly wind, causing frozen fingers! Once the Blenheim's engines were running I would check the radio, R/T, generator and IFF to show that we were friendly aircraft—the last not to be confused with FFI (Freedom from Infection), which routinely involved dropping our trousers while the MO took a good look at us!

We had come from an Army Co-operation squadron and so we had no night-flying experience, but since the Squadron was required to carry out night intruder raids our training involved making innumerable circuits and cross-country flights overnight. Daytime activities involved formation flying and fighter affiliation, where the gunnery leader took charge, flying with the formation leader.

It was not until 27 January 1942 that I went on my first 'op'—to bomb Boulogne docks. It was very cold at 12,000 feet and, although a gunner in a Blenheim was not quite a tail gunner, I still felt isolated. I remember on one occasion when using my radio that I dropped my pencil and took off my gauntlet for a few seconds in order to retrieve it. My fingers began to freeze and I was lucky not to get frostbite.

On 12 February, having just touched down from a blind landing, panic stations erupted. It had been arranged that, should the German battlecruiser *Scharnhorst* escape from hiding, our Blenheims would load with armour-piercing bombs, form up and bomb her from 12,000 feet. However, owing to low cloud, No 110's Blenheims took off singly and headed for the ship. I got really worried as we flew into dense cloud and I could see ice on the wings and tailplane with only the drone of the engines and the dampness in the turret for company.

We must have been at about 10,000 feet before we broke into sunlight. The navigator had worked on dead reckoning and eventually we felt that we

should be somewhere near the target, but in fact we couldn't even see the sea! Radio bearings were useless, so we did a square search and eventually found the sea but no warship. We headed home, and on arrival discovered that the only aircraft to have found the target had been shot down. A few other Blenheims did not get back to Wattisham but, happily, managed to land elsewhere.

Left: The German battlecruiser *Scharnhorst*.

Heavy losses resulted from supporting the Norwegians, and the squadrons returned to Wattisham on 3 May. While the main activity at the airfield was concerned with getting damaged aircraft back 'on line', events in France and the Low Countries meant that the Station was kept extremely busy. When the Nazis invaded those countries from 10 May,

Above: Attending to the nose-mounted machine gun. These rearward-firing weapons were a modification introduced to give the Blenheim crews an extra measure of protection following the serious losses sustained during the early months of the war.

Left: Safely home: the relief is apparent as a Blenheim crew deplane following an attack on enemy targets.

IMPERIAL WAR MUSEUM

BRISTOL BEAUFIGHTER Mk Ic

Type: Strike fighter
Engines: Two supercharged 1,400hp Bristol Hercules XI radials
Length: 41ft 4in (12.60m)
Wing span: 57ft 10in (17.63m)
Speed: 320mph (515kph) maximum
Range: 1,200 miles (1,930km)
Armament: Four fixed 20mm Hispano cannon and six fixed .303 machine guns.
Crew: Two (pilot and navigator)

Opposite: Profiles showing a Boston Mk III of No 226 Squadron (upper) and a Blenheim IV of No 18 Squadron.

Above right: No 236 Squadron's Beaufighter T4800, photographed at Wattisham.

Below: A profile of the same aircraft. As seen here, this was a time of some revision to the colour schemes and style of markings carried by RAF combat aircraft.

May and June 1942 saw further movements, with No 18 Squadron returning and No 13 arriving in order to participate in the 'Thousand-Bomber Raids' on Germany, but the colour of the uniform was about to change: from 12 June 1942 RAF Wattisham, as Station B.12, was to come under the wing of the United States Eighth Air Force. The RAF units were relocated, non-squadron personnel decamping to Feltwell and the squadrons and their aircraft moving to Oulton (No 236), and West Raynham (No 18). All went quiet at Wattisham, but a sleeping giant was about to awaken . . .

No 236 Squadron

Motto
Speculati Nuntiate
('Having Watched, Bring Word')

Equipment
Bristol Beaufighter Mk Ic strike fighters (code letters 'ND')

Right: No 236 Squadron attacking enemy shipping in the English Channel.

IMPERIAL WAR MUSEUM

NEW MANAGEMENT

N O SOONER had the RAF moved out of Wattisham in 1942 than the Americans moved in: refurbished as an Eighth Army Air Force bomber base, it would, in the event, host the 479th Fighter Group, equipped initally with twin-engine, twin-tailed P-38 Lightnings and later with single-engine P-51 Mustangs. New concrete runways were laid and new buildings, with better facilities, were built to replace and enhance those the RAF had used, although the bomb damage to the main hangars was not fully repaired. Three principal runways were constructed, '29/11' some 1,400 yards in length, '34/16' also of 1,400 yards and '24/06' of almost 2,000 yards. Each had a different surface, varying from all-concrete ('29/11'), through concrete and turf ('34/16') to concrete and steel matting ('24/06'). A secondary base, known as Hitcham, was built at the southern edge of the airfield and here was quartered the 4th Strategic Air Depôt; the associated T2-type hangars are still in existence.

Wattisham's first American occupants, for a short spell in late 1942, were the 68th Observation Group flying the Bell P-39D Airacobra. Shortly after this the 10th Air Depot was formed, tasked with the reclamation and repair of damaged bombers. The co-located 3rd Advanced Air Depôt carried out upgrades on P-38s, P-47s and P-51s to ready them for action over Europe.

After nearly eighteen months, the Eighth Air Force located a front-line fighter group at Wattisham. The 479th FG, comprising the 434th, 435th and 436th Fighter Squadrons and equipped with P-38J Lightnings, arrived at the station on 14 and 15 May 1944. The Group was led by Lieutenant-Colonel Kyle F. Riddle and later became known as 'Riddle's Raiders'. Formed the previous October in the United States, the Group, comprising mostly inexperienced pilots, was directed to support the Normandy landings. Its first mission took place on 24 May.

Escorting Eighth Air Force bombers on daylight raids into Europe, the young pilots found themselves up against the best of the Luftwaffe and, initally, paid a heavy price. The P-38 was the first fighter capable of escorting bombers all the way to their targets, but these journeys cost some fourteen pilots their lives in June alone. The missions are remembered by Major Mario Prevosti:

**United States
Eighth Army Air Force**

Headquarters
Savannah Army Air Base, Georgia

479th Fighter Group

Motto
Icimus ut Unum
('We Strike as One')

Original base
Grand Central Air Terminal,
Glendale, California

Radio call-sign
'Highway'

COURTESY JERRY SCUTTS

Opposite: The rear-engined Bell P-39 Airacobra, a type seen in the skies over Wattisham for a brief period late in 1942 when it was operated by the 68th OG.

Above: The first 479th FG aircraft to arrive at Wattisham were twin-tailed Lockheed P-38J Lightnings, an example of which is depicted here.

Right: For two years from June 1942 Wattisham hosted no permanent combat squadrons but the Station was subjected to major renovation and upgrading in preparation for the arrival of the US Eighth Army Air Force. This map shows the extent of the changes and may be compared with that on page 11. The regular dispersals of the three resident Fighter Squadrons are indicated, as is the location of the oddly named Hitcham facility (the village of Hitcham itself being several miles distant).

Map labels:

0   ½
MILES

CHARLES TYE Former Blenheim dispersals
Former Blenheim dispersals

RINGSHALL

Bomb store

434th FS

WATTISHAM

435th FS

RUNWAY 24/06

RUNWAY 34/16

434th FS

Chapel Farm

436th FS

Control tower

RUNWAY 29/11

GREAT BRICETT

Hitcham (4th Strategic Air Depôt)

GREEN STREET GREEN

4th SAD billeting

NEDGING TYE

The Red Lion

One of the Best Airfields in England

Corporal Guy Purdy, Assistant Crew Chief, 434th Fighter Squadron

Our group arrived at Wattisham airfield by train and by truck early in the morning of 15 May 1944. Because it was still dark, we were unable to see what the base looked like. We were taken to the Mess Hall for breakfast; it was the first time I had tasted powdered eggs! When daylight came, we were surprised to discover that we would be billeted in brick barracks, not tents or Quonset huts as was the case on some other USAAF bases. Our immediate thought—how fortunate we were to be stationed at one of the best airfields in England!

I had been assigned to the 434th Fighter Squadron, Flight 'D', and was required to service P-38 Lightning and P-51 Mustang fighter planes; I was the Assistant Crew Chief and was a corporal. Sometimes we would be obliged to sleep in a Quonset hut and every now and then we would hear V-1 flying bombs overhead. We got used to the sound, but on one occasion the sound cut out, which meant that the missile would be coming down somewhere nearby. We all headed for the door, but one of our men, John Stanovich, ran from the end of the hut, jumped over our pot-bellied stove and broke the stove

pipe. Later we learned that we had heard was in fact only the noise of a 6 x 6 Army truck with a broken muffler and not a V-1 at all! Stanovich never lived that down and we all had a good laugh for a long time afterwards.

Another memory is that we had a cook on our squadron who was originally from Los Angeles and made the finest doughnuts you ever tasted, using potato flour and small eggs imported from Denmark. Now that was a real treat for us!

Left: Guy Purdy (centre) and 434th FS ground crewmen Jim Dillon (left) and John Gilchrist pose in front of a P-38 Lightning nicknamed 'No Guts?', Wattisham, 1944.

434th Fighter Squadron

Equipment
Lockheed P-38 Lightning and North American P-51 Mustang fighters (fuselage code 'L2'; radio call-sign 'Newcross')

435th Fighter Squadron

Equipment
Lockheed P-38 Lightning and North American P-51 Mustang fighters (fuselage code 'J2'; radio call-sign 'Lakeside')

436th Fighter Squadron

Equipment
Lockheed P-38 Lightning and North American P-51 Mustang fighters (fuselage code '9B'; radio call-sign 'Bison')

Left: A bombed-up P-38J Lightning with (background) P-51B Mustangs at Wattisham, 1944.

LOCKHEED P-38J LIGHTNING

Type: Long-range escort fighter
Engines: Two 1,425hp Allison V-1710-49/53 inlines
Length: 37ft 10in (11.53m)
Wing span: 52ft 0in (15.85m)
Speed: 410mph (660kph) maximum
Range: 450 miles (725km)
Armament: One 20mm cannon and four 0.5in machine guns, plus up to 1,600lb (725kg) of external fuel or ordnance
Crew: Pilot only

COURTESY HOOSIER AIR MUSEUM

Above right: A P-38J Lightning at Wattisham and wearing 'D-Day' recognition stripes.

Below: Two 479th FG Lockheed P-38Js flown from Wattisham —Donald A. Dunn's Olive Green and Neutral Gray 436th FS Lightning, and 'Sweet Mary' flown by 434th FS pilot Keith E. Canella. Most early USAAF fighters were camouflaged, but in later months, as air superiority was gained over Europe, the aircraft were left in their natural finish—which, incidentally, added a few more miles per hour to their top speed.

Bottom: A wartime scene at Wattisham with P-38s dispersed about the airfield.

'On one mission over Berlin, the sky was just filled with planes— bombers, fighter planes, enemy planes—and all hell broke loose. In the confusion, I looked around and realised that I had become detached from my unit. One of our orders was that if you got detached, you were to head south and pick up the Fifteenth Air Force, who were bombing in Poland. You were to meet them on the Polish border, and escort them back to Italy and then head back home. So I went down and picked them up as a lone escort. When they got just past me and over the Alps, I headed for home. I really tried to conserve my gas because I knew that for a fighter pilot, I had flown an awfully long way. I'll never forget—I was coming in for the landing and my engine quit. I was out of gas! That's how close I was. They had to pull me off the runway. I learned that the others in my group had landed in France due to a lack of fuel returning from the mission to Berlin.'

Another story is told by Lieutenant Flamm D. ('Dee') Harper, who, during the afternoon of 15 July 1944, crash-landed his P-38J in Mont-morrillon, France, a small town some forty miles south-east of the

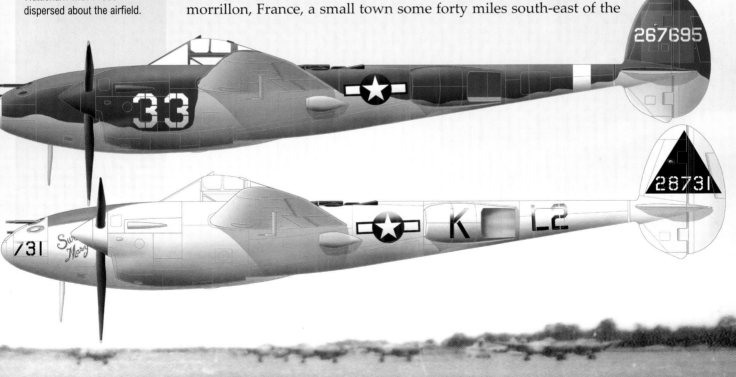

city of Poitiers. It was his twenty-ninth combat mission—an armed reconnaissance and fighter sweep over south central France—and the seventy-ninth flown by the 479th Fighter Group at that time. He was to fly as the 'spare' for the 434th Fighter Squadron, but when the No 3 in First Lieutenant Robin Olds's flight aborted immediately after take-off Harper replaced him as the element leader. After reaching the patrol area, the pilots let down through the clouds, breaking out at about 3,000 feet. They began the attack, and on the second strafing pass, while shooting into a row of 'igloos', a tremendous explosion occurred in front of Harper's fighter. He recounts the tale in the article opposite.

On 29 July 1944 drama came to the 479th with the Allies' first encounter with a German rocket-propelled fighter. Captain Arthur Jeffrey was escorting limping bombers back to the Britain when a Messerschmitt Me 163 Komet was seen to attack one of the them. Jeffrey engaged, and after some extreme manœuvres he managed to land a hit on the

434th Fighter Squadron

Badge adopted following re-equipment of Squadron with P-51 Mustangs

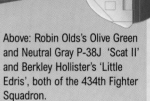

Above: Robin Olds's Olive Green and Neutral Gray P-38J 'Scat II' and Berkley Hollister's 'Little Edris', both of the 434th Fighter Squadron.

Below: Major Donald J. Pierce, the last CO of the 434th FS at Wattisham.

Left: 'Tarzana', a P-38J flown from Wattisham, with its pilot, Lieutenant James L. Wallace of the 434th Fighter Squadron.

US AIR FORCE

COURTESY HOOSIER AIR MUSEUM

Right: P-51s of the 435th Fighter Squadron on a sortie. The aircraft are fitted with long-range fuel tanks under the wings, enabling them to fly deep into enemy territory.

Below: Pilots did not always make it back to base. This P-51 had to be force-landed at Martlesham Heath in September 1944. The pilot, Captain Claire L. Duffié, was unhurt.

Right: Lieutenant Robert B. Kline's 'The Onley [sic] Genevieve IV', another 434th P-51D 'bubble-hood'.

Below: Robert B. Kline in his Mustang. The gun sight is prominent behind the aircraft's windshield

count up its final tally of achievements—351 missions, 155 air-to-air victories and 279 air-to-ground victories. The 479th, which was awarded two Distinguished Unit Citations in August and September 1944, lost a total of 69 aircraft in operations from Wattisham.

The Group departed from the airfield on 22 November 1945, still under the command of Colonel Kyle Riddle, and arrived back in the United States four days later. It could congratulate itself on a job extremely well done.

Right: Hostilities in Europe over, families were able to inspect the 'offices' of their loved ones. The aircraft here is Robert I. Bromschwig's P-51D 'Kraut Knocker'.

Below: P-51 Mustangs fill the camera frame at Wattisham, 1945.

POSTWAR PAUSE

O N 6 JANUARY 1946 Wattisham was returned to
Royal Air Force stewardship. Gloster Meteor
Mk IIIs of the Boxford Wing carried out various
trials to assess the suitability of the Station for jet
aircraft, but the facilities were found wanting and no
permanent establishment was made. Many other
RAF units operated from the airfield over
the course of the next few years, but none
stayed for any length of time. The squadrons
based temporarily at Wattisham, and details of
the aircraft they used, are summarised in the table below.
It became common for De Havilland Vampires operated by
RAF squadrons based in Germany to visit the Station in order
to make use of the nearby East Coast ranges. There were also some
unusual visitors: early in 1951, for example, shortly after permanent
RAF units had moved in once more, Royal Navy Sea Furies from 802
Naval Air Squadron, based at Culdrose, were to be seen flying in the
circuit.

As the Station prepared for the arrival of the Meteors of Nos 263 and
257 Squadrons, much of the infrastructure was improved and renovated,
and in October 1950 Wattisham finally assumed the rôle—sustained for
the next 42 years—of host station of an Air Combat Group.

Wattisham Residents, 1947–1948

Date of arrival	Unit	Equipment	Date of departure
2 January 1947	No 56 Squadron	Meteor III	19 April 1947
	No 266 Squadron	Meteor III	16 April 1947
7 May 1947	No 695 Squadron	Spitfire XVI	20 July 1949
July 1947	Fighter Command School of Technical Training	Oxford, Martinet, Beaufighter, Harvard	July 1949
September 1948	No 601 Squadron	Spitfire 16	September 1948
	No 604 Squadron	Spitfire 16	September 1948

COURTESY PHILIP JARRETT

Main image: The years 1946–1950 saw many comings and goings at Wattisham, but no permanent squadron basing. Among the fighter aircraft resident for short periods were the Gloster Meteor Mk IIIs of No 56 Squadron, normally based at RAF Boxted, which over-wintered for some five months in 1946–47.

Opposite page: Spitfires appeared briefly at Wattisham in the shape of the L.F. Mk XVIs (or 16s—from 1948 all British military aircraft were designated in arabic numerals) of No 604 Squadron, which flew in from RAF Horsham St Faith in 1947.

Right: The Fighter Command School of Technical Training operated a variety of aircraft, including the Miles Martinet (upper photograph) and Airspeed Oxford (lower).

COURTESY PHILIP JARRETT

COURTESY PHILIP JARRETT

COURTESY PHILIP JARRETT

33

METEOR MEMORIES

FOLLOWING a three-year period of relative inactivity while runways were re-laid and new service buildings erected, No 257 Squadron arrived at Wattisham on 27 October 1950, quickly to be joined in November by No 263 Squadron from Horsham St Faith. No 263 was commanded by Squadron Leader J. R. H. Merryfield, whose first claim to fame was that he had at one time held the transatlantic speed record—seven hours out and five hours on the return in a Mosquito, at an average speed of some 450 knots. Somewhat surprisingly for a peacetime establishment, No 263 was allocated a total of 22 aircraft and 32 pilots, although in practice it could never boast these numbers.

Within a short time the Gloster Meteor Mk 4s with which both squadrons were equipped were replaced with Meteor F. Mk 8s. The new version of the aircraft represented a big improvement for the squadrons over its predecessor: it had a greater fuel capacity (and therefore greater range), and in terms of configuration featured a redesigned tail and engine intakes. For the pilots, there was now the reassurance of an ejection seat.

Why is the ejection seat worthy of mention? The answer is that during its history with the Royal Air Force the Meteor had been the dubious possessor of a phenomenal crash record: by 1952, one was being lost, on average, every other day! It is understandable, therefore, that a means of escape would be treated with some interest. Even so, according to some published figures, 312 Meteors equipped with ejection seats crashed, 125 pilots were lost and only 39 successfully ejected.

The arrival in 1952 at the USAF bases in East Anglia of the first F-86 Sabre fighters led to increased competition, rivalry and, surely, a fuller appreciation of the ageing design of the Meteor: RAF pilots were suddenly finding themselves pitched against counterparts with Sabre-versus-MiG-15 experience from the Korean conflict. The British aviation

No 257 (Burma) Squadron
The squadron gifted by the people of Burma during World War II, marked by the Burmese chinthe carried on the coat of arms

Motto
Thay Myay Gyee Shin Shwe Hti ('Death or Glory')

Equipment
Gloster Meteor Mk 4 (1950) and Mk 8 (1950–54), Hawker Hunter Mk 2 (1954–1957, Mk 5 (1955–1957) and Mk 6 (1957)

Below: Nos 257 and 263 Squadrons in immaculate presentation at Wattisham, *circa* 1951. The No 263 Squadron CO's aircraft has its fin and rudders painted dark blue.

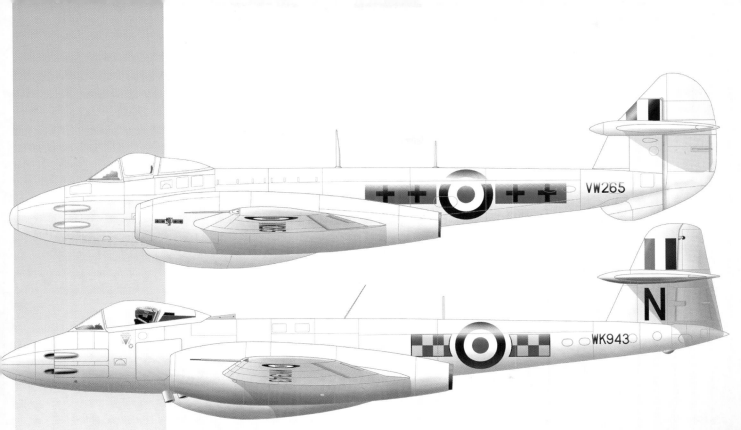

Above: Meteor day interceptor fighters at Wattisham—a Mk 4 of No 263 Squadron (top) and the revised and upgraded Mk 8, this one in No 257 Squadron colours (above). The F.8s were originally in 'silver' finish but by the mid-1950s had acquired camouflage.

Right: Refuelling No 257's Mk 8s at Wattisham in 1950. The 1940s-style coding on the rear fuselage swiftly gave to way to a more colourful display of Squadron markings.

COURTESY 'MAC' MCEWEN

No 263 Squadron
The Squadron's links with
Scotland and Norway are
represented by, respectively,
the lion and the crown

Motto
Ex Ungue Leonem
('By his claws
one knows the lion')

Equipment
Gloster Meteor Mk 4 (1950)
and Mk 8 (1950–55), Hawker
Hunter Mks 2 and 5 (1955–
1957)

Below: Profile of a Meteor Mk 8
of No 263 Squadron.

history of the early 1950s demonstrates the wartime thinking that still permeated the minds of the authorities. Massive, set-piece exercises continued to be staged, and it was as part of one of these that in March 1952 it was decided to bring No 263 Squadron up to its wartime strength and for one week subject Wattisham to 'attack' by Belgian fighters, bombers and paratroops. Shortly after this Merryfield left for Korea, where his second claim to fame was achieved: as well as damaging two Communist MiG-15s, he shot down a US Air Force F-86 that had been abandoned by its pilot but was continuing to circle his parachute!

At home, the years 1952–53 saw the preparations for the Coronation of Queen Elizabeth II, and plans for a huge flypast to celebrate the event, in addition to the Squadrons' normal training routine, kept the airfield personnel busy. A great deal of practice preceded the actual flypast, and, in

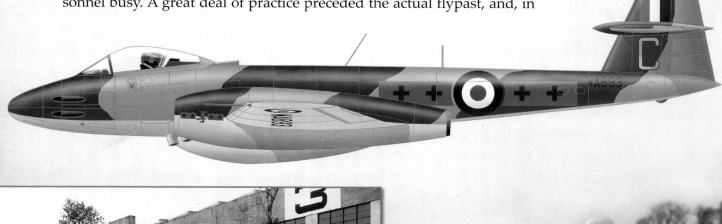

COURTESY WALT FARLEY

GLOSTER METEOR F. Mk 8

Type: Day interceptor fighter
Engines: Two 3,600lb (1,630kg) thrust Rolls-Royce Derwent 8 turbojets
Length: 44ft 7in (13.59m)
Wing span: 37ft 2in (11.33m)
Speed: 600mph (965kph) maximum
Range: 980 miles (1,580km)
Armament: Four 20mm Hispano cannon
Crew: Pilot only

Opposite, top: Personnel of No 257 Squadron in 1954 with one of the unit's Meteor Mk 8s forming the backdrop.

Right, top: Meteor 8s of No 257 Squadron perform a flypast at Wattisham for the Air Officer Commanding, 1950.

Right: Flight Lieutenant David Vernon and his mount at Wattisham in 1950. No 2 hangar, blitzed during the war, is still not fully back in service.

Below: The No 257 Squadron flight line at Wattisham in 1950.

Below, far left: The Station was honoured with a visit by HRH The Duke of Edinburgh shortly after the Meteor squadrons became fully operational. A Meteor Mk 4 of No 263 Squadron is just visible at far left.

COURTESY DAVID VERNON

COURTESY DAVID VERNON

COURTESY DAVID VERNON

Learning the Hard Way

Air Commodore 'Mac' McEwen AFC, *pilot, No 257 Squadron*

Like a host of other young fighter pilots learning about the art of fighter combat in the 1950s and 1960s, I have happy memories of Royal Air Force Wattisham and the surrounding Suffolk countryside. There was something special about Wattisham for everyone, but especially so for me because I did two tours there, the first on No 257 Squadron flying Gloster Meteors and then converting to the Hawker Hunter, my first supersonic aircraft; and the second a few years later on No 56 Squadron converting from the Hunter to the English Electric Lightning, the first aircraft I flew that could reach twice the speed of sound in level flight. Exciting times indeed—and full of what you might call 'character-forming' experiences.

I arrived at Wattisham one wintry Sunday night on 1 February 1954 in a prolonged snowstorm. There were several inches of snow on the roads and the signposts were illegible because ice and snow had stuck to the arms, obliterating the placenames. There were no flat signboards in those days (except on the major roads) and I was taking what I thought would be a short cut anyway, so I was on narrow Suffolk lanes. I had to stop at each signpost and scrape the snow away to read it, but eventually, with some relief, I saw the lights of what was clearly an airfield. However, there appeared to be no way in, and every signpost I laboriously read pointed to Wattisham. Lost already—and I hadn't even arrived yet! Eventually I found a cottage and asked a suspicious-looking local where the entrance was. He directed me, rather grudgingly I thought (perhaps I was a spy or something?), and half an hour later I drew up outside a warm and inviting Officers' Mess. After being cordially greeted by the Orderly Officer and plied with a beer or two, I began to think that Wattisham wasn't such a backwater as I thought it was.

In fact, it was soon evident that this was a busy and thriving fighter base, housing two Meteor day fighter squadrons (Nos 257 and 263 with Mk 8s) and a night fighter squadron (No 152, flying the N.F.11). Each squadron had 24 aircraft and 36 pilots, and the flying rate was considerable as the Meteor was a simple and robust aircraft and one that, unlike the generations of aircraft that succeeded it, rarely went unserviceable. Each squadron was divided into two flights and the flight lines were run by 'Chiefies' (Flight Sergeants or Chief Technicians) who were a law unto themselves. They were mostly strong characters, but kindly men, highly protective of the aircraft entrusted to their care and of the ground crews who serviced them in all weathers with much skill and great cheerfulness. I flew about 400 hours with No 257 Squadron on Meteors and I don't believe that I ever put a Meteor unserviceable, partly because I didn't dare cross swords with the Chiefy but mostly because there was nothing wrong. If only the later types of fighter had been so reliable! If there was a fault, it was usually something minor that could be left until the end of the day for the groundcrew night shift to rectify. They would work until all hours to provide the needed number of aircraft ready to go the next morning, and for a long time I was unaware that while we pilots lived it up in the Mess bar at nights or caroused the Suffolk countryside (The Swan at Lavenham was always a favourite spot) the groundcrew were beavering away to such good intent.

The Royal Air Force had not anticipated fully the implications of the 1950s build-up brought about by the Korean War, and there were inevitably some shortages. Accommodation was one such difficulty, and officers had to share rooms in the messes, which were full to bursting. This is an illustration of how times have changed. When the Prison Service recently tried to overcome the shortage of prison cells by putting two convicts into a cell instead of just one, there was an outcry from the liberalists that this would be an infringement of their human rights! However, it was quite in order in the 1950s to do the same to the nation's officer classes!

Another shortage, which may seem unimportant now but wasn't then, concerned lockers for aircrew. These lockers were large wooden affairs that took up a lot of space in a rather cramped 'changing area' set aside among the hangar offices. When you arrived on a squadron, therefore, the first important thing was to get your name on the waiting list for a locker. I was about tenth on the list and meanwhile was allocated a square yard or so of floorspace under a window which leaked when it rained because the catch was faulty. I had to use this catch to hang my flying suit from, so the suit was often damp before I had even started. Progressing up the waiting list became a major concern, and probably led to the story about the squadron solo aerobatic pilot (each squadron had its own aerobatic low-level display pilot in those days) who announced that he had perfected the art of flying a low-level loop in cloud, so that henceforth his displays would no longer be restricted by the notoriously fickle low cloud that always plagued the summer season. The next time there was a suitable weather day with a cloud base of around 600 feet, therefore, he set off to demonstrate his new bad-weather looping technique and was soon roaring across the field before an admiring crowd of fellow pilots, pulling up sharply in the middle of the runway and entering cloud at a steep angle. There was then a lot of engine noise and the sound of an aircraft accelerating violently before he reappeared, pointing vertically at the ground with not a hope of pulling out in time. The aircraft smashed into the centre of the runway with a terrific impact, followed by a great ball of black smoke. The crowd of pilots looked on in shocked horror, stunned into silence, until an Australian exchange pilot at the back, with a somewhat twisted sense of humour and a very sharp wit called out loudly, 'Christ! What's his locker number?' This remark was not well received by his colleagues at the time, but it does illustrate the anguish brought about by the shortage of lockers.

We used to plan to fly twice in the morning and twice in the afternoon, and so the hours on type and the confidence levels soon built up. In fact, the confidence levels were perhaps a shade too high, because the fatal accident rate on the Meteor was colossal. Figures from the RAF Museum, Hendon, and from squadron diary extracts at the Records Office at Kew show that, in the decade from 1945 to 1955, four hundred Meteor pilots were killed. This is a sobering figure indeed, especially since it occurred during peacetime operations. At the time it was ascribed to a variety of causes, the most common of which appear to have been collisions and loss of control in cloud and accidents occurring while pilots were practising single-engine flying. But there were other causes too, for example, 'Flew into trees while low flying', 'Crashed during unauthorised beat-up', 'Hit sea while in formation', 'Hit cliffs while in formation' and 'Pilot lost on unauthorised night flight'. A fair number of deaths occurred during low-level aerobatics as well.

These were the early years of jet fighter operations, of course, and there was much inexperience at all levels, but the root cause would seem to be to me that there was simply too little supervision. A young pilot was left pretty much to his own devices and he learnt his trade the hard way by coping with new experiences on his own. Things did not always work out well, as many of those 400 pilots discovered. The accident rate could certainly not be blamed on the aircraft, which was inherently safe and a joy to fly. The ejection seats in those days were not as foolproof as they are today, of course, so when things went badly wrong there was often no escape. In the main, however, it was simply because pilots were over-confident and trying to run before they could walk. Fortunately, during the period that I flew Meteors on No 257 Squadron, none of the accidents proved to be fatal, but this was certainly not the case when we re-equipped with Hawker Hunters in early 1955.

the course of this, tragedy struck when two Meteors from No 257 collided, killing Flight Lieutenant Blewitt and Pilot Officer Forrest.

The hard work was revealed on 15 July 1953, when a total of 641 aircraft flew over RAF Odiham in salute to the newly crowned Sovereign; at the same time, on the ground, some 318 aircraft were arranged in static display for review by Her Majesty, No 257 Squadron being represented on the ground by Meteor F.8 WK943/'N' and in the air by twelve aircraft. The flypast took twenty-seven minutes to pass the review point and its like will never be seen again.

The normal round of exercises and detachments kept the Squadrons fully occupied over the ensuing years, until in November 1954 the spotlight fell on No 257 Squadron when it was selected as the first front-line unit to receive the Sapphire-engined Hunter F. Mk 2. No 263 received its new mounts, also Hunter F.2s, the following February.

Above: A No 257 Squadron Meteor pilot stands to attention alongside his mount.

Right: Major Howard N. Tanner, OC No 257 Squadron, discusses with colleagues the unit's unique chinthe insignia on one of its Meteor Mk 8s.

Below: Inspection parade for No 257 Squadron at Wattisham in 1954. Today, fifty-four years on, the same hardstand is occupied by Army Air Corps Apache helicopters.

Commemorating the Greatest Battle

During the 1950s, air shows were one of three different types of event—the Farnborough Air Shows, run by the Society of British Aircraft Companies and held to demonstrate to potential customers, and the public, the latest in British aviation; Armed Forces Days, held at the USAFE bases in Europe with the general theme of 'Come and meet your American neighbors'; and the annual Battle of Britain Open Days, held at almost every RAF station on the Saturday nearest to 15 September, to commemorate the greatest air battle in our history.

Wattisham, being an active fighter station, was busily involved in the Battle of Britain displays, both at the Station itself and in sending representatives elsewhere. These events were very different from the air shows of today, however: for example, there was little or no separation of the crowd from the static aircraft, and there was much more in the way of performance from the home-based squadrons.

A quick look at the advertising for the show held on 18 September 1954 (see opposite) shows that the base was open from 2 p.m. to 6 p.m. and that admission was free (it did cost five shillings to park your car if you were lucky enough to own one), and a bold notice stated, 'We are sorry but you cannot bring a camera'. Permission for such devilish instruments was clearly granted to some, as the photograph below demonstrates!

In the early 1950s, of course, memories of World War II were still fresh in people's minds and aircraft of that era were still to be seen. As so many stations were open on the same day, the RAF would fly formations of similar types to a pattern designed to include a flypast at as many airfields as possible. In East Anglia, one would expect Wattisham, Felixstowe, Honington, Coltishall, West Raynham and Marham all to be open at the same time, and formations of Lincoln bombers, Royal Navy fighters (Attackers in this case), Swifts, Hunters and Britannia transports all appeared in the skies over Wattisham in these days.

Regular items would include Height and Speed Judging, and exhibitions of crazy flying by a local flying instructor in his Auster. As the experimental unit at Martlesham Heath was nearby, the occasional rare gem could appear: at one show Wattisham visitors were fortunate enough to admire the Short Sperrin (an experimental bomber built as an insurance against the failure of the Valiant) and a Lincoln bomber which had a turbojet replacing one of its piston engines. The 'Sound Barrier' was guaranteed to catch the imagination of the public and, if you were lucky, a Hunter or an F-86 Sabre of the US Air Force would swoop and produce a loud double-bang over the field; if you were unlucky, a Meteor would (relatively speaking) trundle past at all of 400 knots, accompanied by two firecrackers exploded from the Tower. The 1955 show included a Sunderland, a Balliol and the first formation team to be seen in East Anglia—a 'four-ship' of Hunters from the home-based No 257 Squadron.

During the latter years of the 1950s, shows started to become more sophisticated and aerobatic teams arrived on the programme. Favourites at

Below: A photograph taken during the 1953 Battle of Britain Open Day at Wattisham. As well as resident Meteors, amongst the aircraft on display are an Airspeed Oxford, a Vampire, a Sabre, a Canberra bomber, a Harvard trainer and, from the USAFE, an F-84G Thunderjet and, looming large in the frame, a B-45 Tornado jet bomber.

Wattisham were the USAFE's 'Skyblazers' team from Bitburg in Germany along with, of course, the 'home team', the 'Black Arrows' of No 111 Squadron. 'Treble One' would generally perform up to three shows on that day—two elsewhere before finishing the show at Wattisham. By the time 'Treble One' flew their last home show, in September 1960, the events were more like those of today, although they were fewer in number. As well as the 'Skyblazers' and the 'Black Arrows', the 20th TFW at Wethersfield provided a twenty-ship flypast of F-100s and a KB-50J tanker flew over while refuelling an F-100, an F-101 and a B-66 Destroyer.

The 1960 show proved to be the last occasion that Wattisham opened its gates to the public on a regular basis. Traffic congestion on the lanes around the Station was becoming a problem and the cost of staging a show were rising. Nationwide, the number of bases hosting such shows began to fall. The year 1968 saw the next event, by which time Wattisham was a supersonic fighter base with two squadrons of Lightnings to provide entertainment, and in the 1972 show international stars in the form of the French aerobatic team 'La Patrouille de France', equipped with Fouga Magisters, were the main attraction. We had to wait nine years for the next show—although that is probably the one that remains to the forefront of the collective local memory most as it featured a flypast by Concorde!

The last full air show at Wattisham was staged in 1989 and featured international participation and a display by the 'Red Arrows'. By now, of course, Wattisham was a Phantom base, but included in the list of aircraft appearing were representatives from Canada, Holland, France and Denmark as well as a good selection from the USAFE. Shows since that year have been limited to small 'Family Days' and low-key events from the now-resident Army Air Corps.

BATTLE OF BRITAIN
(19th Anniversary)

Spend Saturday 19th September
with the ROYAL AIR FORCE at
WATTISHAM AERODROME
2 p.m. to 8 p.m.
ADMISSION FREE
FLYING DISPLAYS
BY JET AIRCRAFT WITH INDIVIDUAL
AND FORMATION AEROBATICS
PASSENGER FLIGHTS BY CONSUL AIRCRAFT
Numerous different types of modern aircraft will be on view
in the static display.
There will also be exhibitions of technical components and
equipment, navigation, meteorology, model aircraft and
safety equipment, with demonstrations of fire-fighting, drill
and model aircraft flying.
Teas and refreshments will be available on the Aerodrome.
Special 'bus services will be operated by the Eastern Counties
'Bus Company, from Ipswich, Stowmarket and Needham
Market, to the airfield. Private coach parties are welcome.
Reduced railway fares to Needham Market are available for
the day. (Consult British Railways for particulars).
Car Parks: Coaches 10s. Cars 5s. Motor-Cycles 2s. 6d.
★ WE ARE SORRY BUT YOU CANNOT BRING A CAMERA

VIA AUTHOR

No 152 Squadron
The crest features the head-dress of the Nizam of Hyderabad

Motto
Faithfully Ally

Equipment
Gloster Meteor N. F. Mk 12 and N. F. Mk 14

As Nos 257 and 263 Squadrons were preparing to receive their new swept-wing Hunters, a separate fighter element was introduced to RAF Wattisham with the recommissioning on 20 June 1954 of No 152 Squadron. Flying radar-equipped Gloster Meteor 12s and 14s, the unit was dedicated to the night fighting rôle and would remain until 28 August 1957.

While the day fighter units of the RAF were equipped with the jet-powered Meteor in the late 1940s and early 1950s, the night fighter units

COLLECTION OF THE LATE HARRY FRYER

Above right: Personnel of No 152 Squadron in 1954 (Squadron Leader Hugh Jones commanding).

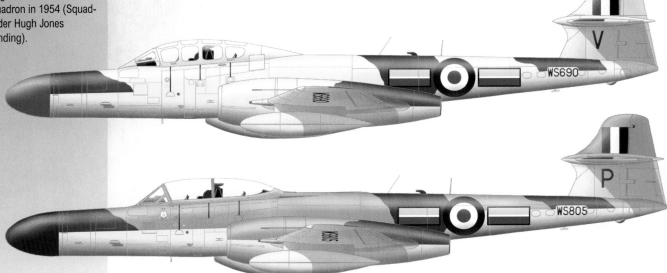

Left: No 152 Squadron's Meteor night-fighters in formation at altitude.

Above: Profiles showing the colours and markings of a No 152 Squadron Meteor N.F.12 (upper) and N.F.14. Amongst other differences, the Mk 12 had a sideways-opening cockpit hood whereas that of the Mk 14 slid backwards for access. The bulge below the fuselage is a conformal external fuel tank.

Right: The work has to go on—even during a severe Wattisham winter.

COURTESY ROB ROOKER

were somewhat ill-equipped with a version of the World War II-era piston-engined Mosquito. In order to equip the RAF with an aircraft comparable to that in use elsewhere in the world—for example, the USAF's F-89 Scorpion—Armstrong Whitworth were tasked with the redesign of Gloster's Meteor to produce a night-fighter version as a 'stand-in' until a more sophisticated aircraft could be built. Known as the N. F. Mk 11, the modified Meteor consisted essentially of a Mk 8 airframe with a modified Mk 7 trainer cockpit to permit the accommodation of a second crew member to operate the AI.10 radar, the latter being installed in an elongated nose. The cannon armament was, as a result, relocated in the wings outboard of the engine nacelles. It took Armstrong Whitworth but a few weeks to get a prototype into the air, and production N. F. 11s totalled 338 airframes and equipped sixteen squadrons.

COURTESY HOWARD N. TANNER

A redesign of the Mk 11 brought about the Mk 12—recognisable by its slightly longer nose and the addition of a fairing around its fin/tailplane 'bullet'. This mark also flew the ultimate version of the Rolls-Royce Derwent engine, the Mk 9. In the nose was a US-designed radar, the West-inghouse APS-21, and its associated cooling unit.

A Mk 13 version of the Meteor (a Mk 11 with a higher specification) followed before the final variant, the Mk 14, arrived in 1953. Equipped with all the improvements recom-mended from the earlier marks, the N. F. 14 was capable of a performance similar to that of the Mk 8 day fighter, with a top speed of around Mach 0.85, and featured an improved cockpit environment, including a clear, one-piece canopy and a strengthened windshield.

ARMSTRONG WHITWORTH METEOR N.F. Mk 12

Type: Night fighter
Engines: Two 3,800lb (1,720kg) thrust Rolls-Royce Derwent 8 turbojets
Length: 49ft 11in (15.22m)
Wing span: 43ft 0in (13.11m)
Speed: 540mph (870kph) maximum
Range: 920 miles (1,480km)
Armament: Four 20mm Hispano cannon
Crew: Pilot and navigator

Left: The Meteors of RAF Wattisham over Trafalgar Square, participating in the Battle of Britain Flypast on 15 September 1954.

Below left: The reason for that long nose: a Meteor N. F. Mk 14 of No 152 Squadron reveals its secrets.

COURTESY ROB ROOKER

ARMSTRONG WHITWORTH METEOR N.F. Mk 14

Type: Night fighter
Engines: Two 3,800lb (1,720kg) thrust Rolls-Royce Derwent 9 turbojets
Length: 51ft 4in (15.65m)
Wing span: 43ft 0in (13.11m)
Speed: 540mph (870kph) maximum
Range: 920 miles (1,480km)
Armament: Four 20mm Hispano cannon
Crew: Pilot and navigator

Right: No 152 Squadron in informal pose. Each aircraft required a crew of two, pilot and navigator, the duties of the latter including also the operation of the radar equipment.

Right and below: The Wattisham flight line with No 152 Squadron centre stage. In the photograph below, the Station's new day fighter equipment—Hawker Hunters—can be seen in the background.

HUNTER HEAVEN

FIGHTER Command took an enormous leap forward in design performance with the demise of the Meteor and its replacement with the Hunter. RAF Wattisham was to become synonymous with the Hunter for many years, but the early period of service for this undoubted Hawker thoroughbred was not an easy time.

Any history involving the Hunter has to be seen in the light of the performance difficulties that were to beset the Mk 1 on its entry into service, although it was somewhat fortunate, to say the least, that foresight had led to the production of two options in terms of both the aircraft that was to become the Command's new, high-performance, swept-wing day fighter (the Swift and the Hunter) and the engine that was to power it (the Avon and the Sapphire).

In the early Hunter, the Royal Air Force found itself with an impotent fighter, its shortcomings caused by engine surges in the early Rolls-Royce

Left: A Hunter F. Mk 2 of No 263 Squadron outside one of the main hangars at Wattisham. Its arrival seems to have been eagerly anticipated!

Below: The Wattisham Hunter wing—all 24 aircraft of both squadrons, Nos 257 and 263— over Orfordness early in1955. Orford itself is centre left.

46

Left: Six Hunters of No 257 Squadron *en echelon* during a sortie over East Anglia.

Right: No 257 Squadron pilots return to the crew room for debrief after a sortie. The two day fighter squadrons based at the Station in the 1950s, equipped first with Meteors and then with Hunters, enjoyed a long and friendly rivalry.

COURTESY HOWARD N. TANNER

Below: No 263's Hunter F.2s undergoing line maintenance preparatory to a sortie. Only a few dozen Mk 2s were built, and Nos 257 and 263 Squadrons both started to receive the improved Mk 5 very shortly after first taking delivery of their new swept-wing jets.

Bottom: Engine start for No 257 Squadron, the aircraft yet to receive their unit markings

Avon whenever the aircraft fired their cannon. The Hunter also suffered from the common British design fault of too limited a fuel capacity: the endurance of the Mk 1 was of the order of forty minutes!

Up at RAF Leuchars, Fife, No 43 (F) Squadron received its first Hunter Mk 1s in July 1954 and was fully equipped two months later, but over the ensuing weeks the RAF lost a total of 37 of the 139 Mk 1s built in flying accidents, some fifteen of which were fatal. At the same time, the alternative fighter, the Supermarine Swift, had been issued to No 56 Squadron at Waterbeach and, knee-deep in its own problems, was proving to be an even bigger failure as a fighter. The insurance policy was

COURTESY ROGER LINDSAY

COURTESY N. TANNER

Scrambled at Sundown

Colonel Howard N. Tanner USAF, Officer Commanding, No 257 Squadron

During the Korean War, forces of the British Commonwealth were introduced into the conflict by being attached to various units already in action. During 1951 the decision was made to bring all of the Commonwealth Forces into an activated 1st British Commonwealth Division under the Command of General Cassels. At that time I was the Operations Officer of a USAF fighter squadron in Korea, and the fact that it was my second tour, and because I was a graduate of the Military Academy at West Point, New York, contributed to my being assigned to the 1st British Commonwealth Division as its first USAF Air Liaison Officer.

I was instructing USAF pilots in the F-86 Sabre jet for combat in Korea when I received a telephone call from the Pentagon offering an Exchange assignment with the RAF as a Squadron Commander. Of course, without hesitation, I accepted. When my family and I arrived at RAF Wattisham I noted that the Commanding Officers were as diverse as those in the 1st British Commonwealth Division. The Station Commander was an Australian, Group Captain H. I. Edwards VC; the Wing Commander was a South African, C. Scott Vos DFC; the No 263 Squadron Commander was a Scot, 'Jock' Aytoun; and Squadron Leader Snyder, English, commanded No 152 Squadron.

Soon after my arrival on No 257 Squadron, I learned that the RAF were in the habit of making night deployments by single aircraft, and so I requested permission, and received approval, to train the Squadron pilots in night formation flying. This training paid off during a London Defense Exercise with two flights of the Squadron on alert. The pair were 'scrambled' at sundown, but shortly after the flights took off RAF Wattisham was closed because of fog—as indeed were all RAF stations except Duxford. Fortunately the flights were able to get to RAF Duxford before it closed and receive landing instructions, but the Tower Controller was astonished to see eight aircraft on the runway instead of only two!

The Squadron was called on to perform many times. The most notable occasions were the visits of the Shah of Persia and the Pakistani Minister of Defense, the Graduation Exercises at RAF Cranwell, the two Squadron flights over London and the low-level flights for radar calibration.

When the RAF Wattisham and RAF Leuchars Wings completed the transition from Meteor 8s to Hawker Hunters, the Leuchars Wing came to Suffolk for a combined Squadron fly-over from RAF Wattisham to London and return. I was honored to be selected to lead the formation of the two Wings.

Other memories include the Squadron visits to The Swan in Lavenham, where on one occasion this non-beer-drinking person downed a yard of ale in thirty seconds; making aileron rolls at 55,000 feet in a Hunter F.2; the birth of our fourth son, who was named Thomas after Wing Commander Thomas John Watkins DSO; learning to play cricket (!); and playing basketball with the Wing basketball team. My family and I made many civilian friends, too, while we were at Wattisham. Among these were Sir George and Lady Falconer, who were frequent visitors to the Station; Mr and Mrs Rupert Cooper from Bricett Hall; Mr Foster, who told me about the USAF 479th Fighter Group being stationed at RAF Wattisham and its being credited with shooting down a jet propelled V-1 bomb; and the ever-helpful Mr Green in the Ipswich Antique Shop.

At the end of my exchange I returned to the United States on board the USNS *General William O. Darby*. As the ship left Southampton, a flight of Hunters from RAF Wattisham flew over to say goodbye. This was—and continues to be—a highly emotional event for me.

HAWKER HUNTER F. Mk 2

Type: Interceptor fighter
Engines: One 8,000lb (3,640kg) thrust Armstrong Siddeley Sapphire ASSa6 turbojet
Length: 45ft 10½in (13.98m)
Wing span: 33ft 8in (10.26m)
Speed: 715mph (1,150kph) or Mach 0.95 maximum
Range: 700 miles (1,120km)
Armament: Four 30mm Aden cannon
Crew: Pilot only

COURTESY HOWARD N. TANNER

Below: Major Howard N. Tanner, OC No 257 Squadron during the transition from Meteor to Hunter, in the cockpit of his Hunter Mk 2 at Wattisham.

COURTESY HOWARD N. TANNER

COURTESY HOWARD N. TANNER

Right: No 257 Squadron's new swept wings. It can be see that the aircraft nearest the camera, 'R', has yet to have its chequerboard insignia completed!

Below: Aircraft as far as the eye can see: all 24 of Wattisham's Hunters, photographed in 1955.

COURTESY HOWARD N. TANNER

COURTESY HOWARD N. TANNER

the Hunter Mk 2, which was fitted with the powerful Armstrong Siddeley Sapphire engine. The Wattisham Wing was to be the first to equip—No 263 Squadron in late 1954 and No 257 in early 1955. Wattisham's love affair with the Hunter had begun.

However, as Air Commodore 'Mac' McEwen recalls, 'not only was the Hunter late in arriving, but it also had a number of defects when it eventually did so. Mk 1 Hunters, with a Rolls-Royce Avon engine, were delivered to No 43 Squadron at Leuchars and Mk 2s, powered by the Armstrong Siddeley Sapphire engine, were issued to No 257 Squadron

Right: No 257 Squadron taxying, the CO's aircraft leading. The aircraft are Mk 5s and feature Aden cannon 'blisters'.

COURTESY HOWARD N. TANNER

Left: Two Hunters of No 257 Squadron, their undercarriage gear almost retracted, leave Wattisham's main runway on a 'scramble'.

Right: No 257 Squadron's pilots pose proudly alongside some of their new mounts. Three of the old Meteor 8s and two more Hunters can be seen in the background.

COURTESY HOWARD N. TANNER

Supersonic Ejection

The Author

AUTHOR'S COLLECTION

In the far-off days of the 1950s there was still some mystique about what had become known to the public as 'the sound barrier'. In reality there was no 'barrier', merely an increase in air resistance as an aircraft approaches the speed of sound. Aircraft design and the increase in aeronautical knowledge at the time had enabled man to progress from a position where exceeding the speed of sound—Mach 1—was impossible (by straight-wing jets especially) to a point where, in a dive, aircraft such as the American F-86 Sabre and the British Hunter could surpass this speed. The use of the word 'barrier' was encouraged by the accompanying double bang of pressure waves heard and felt as an aircraft exceeded this speed. In the middle of the decade, it was common for Hunter pilots to exceed Mach 1, again in a dive, as part of their flying training, learning the stick and aileron forces experienced at high Mach number.

So it was that, on 3 August 1955, a young Flying Officer Hedley Molland, from No 263 Squadron, found himself in a steep dive off the coast near Felixstowe with an indicated air speed in excess of Mach 1. Although he is quite sanguine about it now, one can only guess at the thoughts that raced through his mind on finding that he could not pull out of that dive—which was getting ever steeper. Sense prevailed, however, and he put his body in the hands of Martin Baker, pulled the ejection-seat handle and baled out. In so doing, he entered the history books as the first RAF pilot to bale out at a supersonic speed, and only the second in history (the first being an American F-100 test pilot).

The most astounding story of the jet

I BALED OUT THROUGH THE SOUND BARRIER

It could happen to any R.A.F. pilot. At supersonic speed . . . too late to bale out. At

Pilot Bales Out Above 700 mph
At 25,000 Feet—And Lives

SOUND BARRIER 'MIRACLE'

"*Star*" Reporter

FOR THE FIRST TIME IN THE HISTORY OF SUPERSONIC FLYING IN BRITAIN A PILOT IS BELIEVED TO HAVE ABANDONED HIS AIRCRAFT ON THE OTHER SIDE OF THE SOUND BARRIER AND LIVED

My Supersonic Bale-Out

Only two men have lived through it. Last month we reported on American George Smith; now here's the

tered on my returning consciousness, I wouldn't have stood much of a chance in

COURTESY HEDLEY MOLLAND

From a position of total obscurity, this young man found himself in all the national newspapers and aviation journals. With quite serious wounds to his limbs and lower body, he was picked up by a small vessel sailing close to his splash-down, spending only a few minutes in the water. He was then transferred to Ipswich Hospital, where he was fortunate enough to meet the lady who would become his wife. It was six months before Molland was able to return to active flying duties at Wattisham.

As if one ejection were not enough, on 29 September 1965 our now somewhat experienced ejectee, now a Flight Lieutenant on No 111 Squadron, found his Lightning Mk 3 XP739 indicating unexpected critically low fuel while he was recovering to Wattisham. His knowledge told him of the severity of his situation and he called the Wattisham tower for a priority landing. It was during this radio call that he not only saw 'bingo' lights but heard both of his Rolls-Royce Avons spooling down.

Over the village of Mendlesham, but pointing away from the population, Molland decided that this was not the place to be and he once more pulled the ejection-seat handle. Everything worked as planned and the pilot quickly found himself safely on the ground while the trusty Lightning continued on approach to Wattisham before finally meeting its end at Battisford Hall, not a country mile from the approach to Runway 23. A quick glance at Flight Lieutenant's log book for this day merely reveals the word 'Ejected' and the next entry shows a return to flying three days later.

Now living in Ipswich after a career that took him from the RAF to flying Lightnings in Saudi Arabia, Hedley Molland assures your author that there were no further ejections!

Heading photograph: A Hunter Mk 5 of No 263 Squadron.
Above: The 1950s were times of great excitement in the aviation world, and in those days the Press took up the cause with enthusiasm, reporting with prominence, and at length, the activities of the Royal Air Force—in particular anything relating to supersonic flight and the fabled 'sound barrier'. Flight Lieutenant Hedley Molland's exploit duly made headline news, as indicated by the cuttings here, in one of which he is shown holding a model of a Supermarine Swift (!).
Right: Flight Lieutenant Molland, No 263 Squadron, in his Hunter at Wattisham, strapped to the Martin Baker ejection seat, —equipment that would save his life.

COURTESY HEDLEY MOLLAND

COURTESY REG WYNESS

Opposite, upper: The 'Black Arrows', in Diamond Five formation, hone their skills.

Above: Formation perfection in line abreast.

Below: A No 111 Squadron 'Black Arrows' Hunter F. Mk 6 in profile.

and the public at large. Magazines such as *Flight*, *The Aeroplane*, *Air Pictorial* and *RAF Flying Review* carried photo-reports of the superb formations flown by this team, to a standard that was to become the yardstick against which all future aerobatic teams would be compared (and found lacking).

So it was that, one sunny afternoon in July 1958, local residents suddenly noticed a big arc of white smoke climbing into the skies over Wattisham: 'Treble One' had arrived! Led at this time by Squadron Leader Roger Topp, the team were to become adopted by the Suffolk public in a way that no other RAF unit had been before. Practices by the (then) nine-strong team of glossy black Hunters became the normal daily routine for the Squadron—and the cause of many

The 'Black Arrows' Come to Wattisham

Air Commodore Roger L. Topp AFC**, Officer Commanding, No 111 (F) Squadron

My introduction to RAF Wattisham came about in January 1955. Until then, although I was familiar with the aircraft of Fighter Command, I had little knowledge of the Command's operating procedures and battle tactics. A few days earlier I had been posted from the Royal Aircraft Establishment, Farnborough, to RAF North Weald to take command of No 111 (F) Squadron equipped with Meteor 8s. On arrival at North Weald I found that the Squadron was absent on detachment to Acklington, where they were undertaking a month's concentrated air-to-air gunnery practice. It was sensibly decided that, before taking over the Squadron, I should spend a week of familiarisation with another squadron engaged on normal operational flying duties. Hence I found myself at Wattisham, attached to No 41 Squadron, commanded by 'Jock' Aytoun and whose senior Flight Commander was Pete Latham. Pete took me under his wing, so to speak, and I had a very enjoyable week, learnt a lot but realised I still had a lot to learn. My brief stay over, I left to join my squadron at Acklington, little knowing that some three years later Pete and I would once more come together—and again at Wattisham.

A few months after returning from Acklington to North Weald, No 111 (F) Squadron re-equipped with the Hunter Mk 4, and with this magnificent mount under us we soon decided that, as well as performing all our operational flying duties, we would engage in some light relief doing formation aerobatics. About a year later, and now equipped with the more powerful Hunter Mk 6, we were chosen to represent the RAF as its premier aerobatic team. The 'Black Arrows' were born.

Thus we continued happily at North Weald until late 1957, when it was announced that, because of the increase in commercial air traffic, an airway was to be established passing directly overhead the airfield. This duly came into being, with a lower limit of 3,000 feet. Although this was sufficient for us to complete a formation loop, to do so would be at least controversial, and in any case wrong in principle. To continue with the frequent, close-to-the-ground practice training flights that were necessary to keep the team on the top line and ready for displays, we had to take off from North Weald, fly to Duxford, wait for the circuit to be cleared for ten minutes, go through our routine and then return to base. This proved to be most unsatisfactory: a lot of transfer flight fuel was consumed, we had no team critics on the ground, and unless we carried drop tanks (which were unrepresentative of our display configuration) we could carry out only one practice display routine per sortie.

My misgivings for this unsatisfactory state of affairs were sympathetically received by the C-in-C Fighter Command, Sir Tom Pike, who decided that we should relocate, and before long we learned that our future home would be RAF Wattisham, However, for the moment the airfield there was closed for major repairs to the runway, and so in the meantime we were to go to RAF North Luffenham in Rutland. We were the only squadron at that airfield, and we spent a happy spring and early summer of 1958 giving displays wherever required and trying out ideas for the forthcoming Farnborough Air Show.

On 17 June 1958, despite protestations from air traffic control that the airfield was still 'closed' I flew into RAF Wattisham for the first time since I had been there with Pete

COURTESY REG WYNESS

Latham in January 1955. The Squadron was due to move there from North Luffenham the next day, and I felt that I had better inspect what was to be the Squadron's hangar and working accommodation. I was busy going from room to room with a stick of chalk and muttering to myself, 'This is okay for "B" Flight Commander's office, this will do for the aircrew, this is great for the ground crew, I'll take this one,' etc., when there was a presence and a voice at my elbow. 'We're closed. Just what are you doing here?' demanded the voice. I turned to see an irate Group Captain looking far from pleased.

The Group Captain turned out to be the Station Commander, Teddy Morris, the younger brother of the famous 'Zulu'. He made it abundantly clear that I had contravened endless regulations such as landing without fire or ambulance cover, on an unswept runway, with no ground crew and with no refuelling—and, above all, I had failed to obtain his personal permission—but then his blue eyes twinkled, his legendary good nature took over and he merrily helped me to allocate the rest of the accommodation. I also heard from him the good news that my old friend 'Jock' Aytoun was to be the Wing Commander Flying We parted on good terms, he allowing me to take off from his 'closed' airfield without demur and receiving from me a promise that Wattisham would have a full aerobatic display the next day, the official day for our move. On 18 June 1958 No 111(F) Squadron, incorporating the 'Black Arrows', flew into their new long-term home.

We quickly settled in, both on the Station and in the local area, which we found much to our liking. It was fun to be back on a unit where we were not alone: at North Weald we had been the only squadron there once the two Meteor auxiliary squadrons had disbanded, and at Luffenham we again had

Above: The 'Black Arrows' in Diamond Nine.
Left: A unique document: the page from the Flight Authorisation Book showing twenty-two names and initials for the Farnborough Air Show display on 4 September 1958.

COURTESY REG WYNESS

had the place to ourselves. Now we were sharing the airfield with No 41 Squadron equipped with Javelins, so there were aircraft, aircrew and ground crew aplenty. The messes were very lively places, and friendly inter-squadron rivalry was swiftly in full flow. We also discovered that the smoking chimneys at Claydon—although doubtless not appreciated by many local residents—were a wonderful navigation aid for us: in bad weather, if we could see the smoke we could find the airfield.

With so many people on the station, married quarters were in short supply and many families of all ranks spread far and wide in search of suitable accommodation to rent. But it all worked smoothly enough, the local people being friendly and helpful—and indeed, I believe, rather proud of 'their' airfield and of those who served there. We also quickly found our own particular local leisure facilities, in addition to the many good pubs. For me, it was the golf course near Martlesham Heath.

For the 'Black Arrows', the clock was now ticking rapidly: it was mid-June, and still we had not decided what speciality if any, we should display at Farnborough, which was scheduled for the first week of September. Sir Tom Pike, the C-in-C, had already given me his provisional approval to put on a show with more than our own sixteen aircraft—provided, of course, that whatever we proposed he would permit.

At Farnborough a year earlier we had flown our Diamond Nine formation for the first time, and since then our standard fair-weather display always began with a diamond roll and loop from which four aircraft would 'bomb-burst' away, leaving our standard five to complete the more intricate man-oeuvres. We knew that for 1958 we could introduce the impressive sight of a Diamond Sixteen looping and rolling before bomb-bursting down to nine, etc. However, I had one major reservation: our total complement of aircraft was sixteen, so we had no spares should we encounter any of the unserviceability that for high-performance fighter aircraft is a fact of life from time to time.

COURTESY REG WYNESS

I had one remaining ambition for the 'Black Arrows'. I already had Sir Tom's approval to do something with more than sixteen if we could demon-strate that it was safe, looked good and could be repeated for each of the seven days of Farnborough—which meant that the formation should be reasonably within the capability of the aircraft's performance and that of the pilots. After much soul-searching, theory evolved into airborne trials, during which we would fly various formation outlines or envelopes so that there were

aircraft at all the most difficult station extremities but without filling in the easier formation positions. In addition, using our sixteen aircraft, we could split a trial formation in half, fly that half and then change pilots to fly the other half. The people of Suffolk must have been completely mystified at witnessing their air force flying indescribable formations and performing weird antics in their otherwise peaceful skies.

I had already decided that we should fully exploit one characteristic of a modern jet fighter. For such an aircraft, a loop is nothing more than flying straight and level with a high percentage of engine power set, applying an appropriate amount of 'g', being careful not to apply too much near the apex of the loop and then easing off the 'g', so that straight and level flight is regained at the original altitude. If the engine is suitably powerful and the loop not too 'tight', this procedure can be repeated at will so that the aircraft advances along its course in a succession of loops. Taking this a little further, pilots find that formating while flying straight and level is easy after a little practice—and the 'Black Arrows' had practice aplenty! So a mass loop became the obvious thing to do; in fact, we eventually settled on two consecutive loops.

For the actual formation, we finally decided on what has become known as the 'Twenty-Two', a broad arrow with a frontage of seven aircraft, their pilots looking inwards to maintain station and the remainder flying line astern of the front seven. Sir Tom gave his approval and orders to other squadrons to assist us, and soon the 'borrowed' aircraft arrived and the new pilots were welcomed, rapidly trained and became 'Black Arrows'. Come the Farnborough Air Show, we duly delivered the double loop to open our daily display, following which we also introduced our Diamond Sixteen roll and loop before continuing similarly to the 1957 sequence. At the time we believed that our mass loop with twenty-two operational fighter aircraft (not stunt planes), and at an International Air Show, probably established a world record. Nearly fifty years on, the surviving 'Black Arrows', of whom (as I write) most are still alive, believe this still to be true.

The Farnborough week behind us, we returned to Wattisham to complete the remaining shows of the 1958 season and—dread of dreads—to learn my fate. My time with 'Treble One' was nearly over. I flew my final sortie from Wattisham on 18 October and then handed command of the Squadron and the leadership of the 'Black Arrows' over to none other than Pete Latham, the friend whom I had first met at Wattisham some three years earlier. It was nice to keep it in the family!

Top right: A treat never to be repeated: the 'Black Arrows' (with help from friends) demonstrate their 22-aircraft formation display.
Above: The 'Black Arrows' pilots—in '22' formation—at RAF Odiham.
Right: A 'Treble One' Hunter on display at Wattisham's Battle of Britain Open Day in September 1958. A US Air Force F-100 Super Sabre from Wethersfield is alongside and one of No 41 Squadron's Javelins beyond that.

COURTESY PHILIP JARRETT

COURTESY PHILIP JARRETT

after-hours detentions for the author at the nearby Grammar School at Stowmarket, from where (to the detriment of scholastic pursuits) the view was outstanding.

The number of aircraft in the team soon started to increase. Take-offs would now include standard camouflaged Hunters from the sister squadron at Wattisham, No 56, until, one day in early September, Suffolk was treated to a sight never be forgotten by anyone who witnessed it. Breaking through some light cloud and preceded by a huge roar, no fewer than twenty-two Hunters, in a massive arrow-headed formation descended from a loop. By the following week's Farnborough show the formation had been seen a number of times but it stands today, still, as a record in terms of the number of aircraft executing this manœuvre. Bearing in mind the practice nowadays of equipping aerobatic teams with training aircraft and the costs involved in maintaining them, to say nothing of the stringent rules governing display flying, it seems unlikely that this record will ever be broken.

The loop was to be the swansong for Roger Topp as No 111 Squadron's leader, but not before he was awarded a second bar to his Air Force Cross in recognition of his work with the team. Squadron Leader Peter Latham joined 'Treble One' as the new 'Boss' and, if anyone had fears otherwise, maintained the extraordinarily high standards that had been set by his predecessor. No 111 was by now incorporating the idea of splitting the formation into two smaller teams, always having one in front of the spectators and holding their attention while the other repositioned itself (an innovation often credited, wrongly, to the team's successors, the 'Blue Diamonds' of No 92 Squadron). The year 1959 saw a team of sixteen Hunters at Farnborough and the 'At Home' displays of that September. The second team of seven was lead by squadron veteran Les Boyer, while Latham led the nine-ship formation. After carrying out some large

Above: The immaculate displays of the 'Black Arrows' were performed by equally immaculate aircraft, as this close study shows. A second Hunter can just be seen peeling off well aft.

Above: More 'Black Arrows' perfection—five line abreast and *en echelon*.

Bottom: The arrival of the Hunter did not spell the end of Meteors at Wattisham: No 111 Squadron, for example, used this two-seat T.7 trainer as a 'maid of all work' into the 1960s

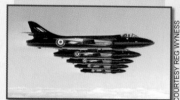

COURTESY REG WYNESS

Above: A poignant memory: No 257 Squadron's disbandment flypast at RAF Wattisham, 29 March 1957.

formation manœuvres, the team would split into two for the second half of the display, joining up to sixteen aircraft again for the finale. It has to be remembered that many of the formations and manœuvres flown by the 'Black Arrows'—Diamond Nine, Wineglass, Apollo (then known as Draken) etc.—were being seen for the first time, although they were taken up by other teams in later years.

The year 1960 saw the team in the headlines again, but not for all the right reasons. In a practice on the morning of 10 June the team were seen to pull up into the final loop and break for landing. The author then saw one Hunter emerge from cloud tail first, to crash near the airfield. No ejection occurred, and aerobatics claimed the life of Flight Lieutenant Stan Wood, a veteran of the team since 1957 and a member of the 22-loop. In the best traditions of the Service, the team were practising again in the afternoon.

If it were possible, a second announcement had an even greater effect on the air-minded public: the 'Black Arrows' were to disband at the end of the 1960 season! The news hit the local residents (not to speak of the local spotters) like a hammer blow: it had never been considered that, one day, there would not be a team at Wattisham. The pilots had gained what would today be considered 'celebrity' status, opening events and making guest appearances in a way never before known (if all too common today). National newspapers soon carried the news that No 92 Squadron were to take over the role. For the final season, Latham added a further two Hunters to the team, which then flew two formations of nine, the second under Brian Mercer, who was to become leader of the following year's

Above: The colourful nose insignia of a No 56 Squadron Hunter.

Below: By the time No 56 Squadron had been relocated to RAF Wattisham, its Hunter 5s had been phased out and replaced by Mk 6s, one of which is depicted in this profile.

No 92 team. By now, for the second season, 'Treble One' was being led by an all-black Hunter T.7.

Complementing 'Treble One' at Wattisham during this period were No 56 Squadron—a unit that would continue its association with the Station into the 1990s and, distinctively, complete tours with three different aircraft types during its tenancy. Arriving in July 1959 from RAF Waterbeach after a disastrous spell on the Supermarine Swift but now with Hunter Mk 6s, the unit made up the second of the standard two day-fighter units with No 111 Squadron, indulging in friendly rivalry but also offering considerable assistance with the business of aerobatic displays. No 56's Hunters were not seen in the skies over Wattisham for long, however, because shortly after the September 1960 'At Home' displays, all the Hunters were posted away and the airfield awaited the arrival of the 'Thunder Beast' from English Electric.

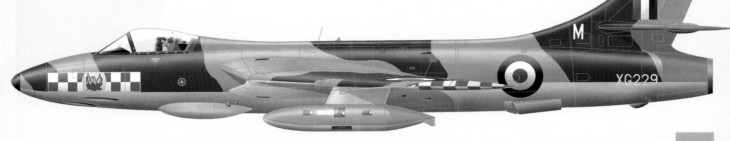

XG229

SEEK AND DESTROY

WITH the demise of the Meteor wings and the arrival of the Hunter day fighter came the need for a new night/all-weather fighter. The Royal Air Force had selected the Gloster Javelin (rather than the De Havilland D.H. 110, which went on to be developed for the Royal Navy as the Sea Vixen) to fulfil the rôle. Thus, in the summer of 1957, No 41 Squadron arrived at Wattisham with Javelin Mk 4s and a single T.3 trainer. The Mk 4 was an improvement over the original Javelin Mk 1, mainly in featuring an all-flying tailplane, but its armament was the same—four 30mm Aden cannon. In terms of its 'punch', however, the Javelin was to be subjected to radical change.

A further improvement was the mounting of rows of razor-like vortex generators on the upper surfaces of the wing, in order to improve the aircraft's handling in the air, although this led to an increased enthusiasm amongst aircrews to vacate their aircraft should they encounter problems on the ground. Hitherto, fire crews were in the habit of lifting the airmen out of the cockpit and sliding them down the wing, but the thought of the effect of sliding over a row of vertical razor blades encouraged many a pilot and navigator to leap to the ground and risk ankle injury!

There was probably never a more distinctive-looking aircraft than the Javelin, with its delta wing and a similarly configured tailplane. The noise generated by the two Armstrong Siddeley Sapphire turbojets was also distinctive, so much so that any need visually to identify the aircraft became redundant.

November 1959 saw the arrival of the Javelin Mk 8 on the Squadron, the improvements incorporated into which were major and very obvious. It was, for example, the first RAF warplane to have missiles as its primary weapon. Now armed with four heat-seeking air-to-air Firestreaks, fitted with re-heated Sapphire engines and equipped with an autopilot and with an uprated radar/target acquisition kit, the Javelin at last reached its potential. According to some sources, it was faster than the Hunter Mk 6 at altitudes over 20,000 feet.

Thus equipped, No 41 Squadron formed a five-ship display team to perform at the annual Battle of Britain 'At Home' displays. The team was known as the 'Flat-Irons ' and, it must be admitted, the aircraft conducted

No 41 (F) Squadron

The Squadron crest originated as the Arms of St-Omer in France, No 41's original headquarters

Motto
Seek and Destroy

Equipment
Gloster Javelin F.A.W Mk 4 (1957–1959), F.A.W. Mk 8 (1959—1963)

Above: The delta-wing Javelin had one of the most distinctive shapes of all postwar jet aircraft. This No 41 example has its four missile pylons vacant.

Above: A Javelin F.A.W.8 of No 41 Squadron based at Wattisham, showing the aircraft's primary armament of four Firestreak heat-seeking missiles.

Right: The Mk 8s replaced the earlier Mk 4s, one of which is seen here. The aircraft's call-sign, painted in the tailfin, comprised the three numerals of the serial number; these were later replaced with a single-letter call-sign.

Below: No 41 Squadron's Javelin Mk 8s prepare for take-off at Wattisham. The Hunter day fighters await their turn in the background.

themselves somewhat more sedately than their Hunter neighbours in Hangar 1! David Octon recalls: 'During that period the Squadron was busy providing air defence of the United Kingdom, our aircraft armed with Firestreak missiles and four 30mm Aden cannon. In August 1961, at the time of the Cuban Missile Crisis, we were detached to Geilenkirchen in

COURTESY WATTISHAM AIRFIELD MUSEUM

COURTESY DAVID SEWARD

GLOSTER JAVELIN F.A.W. Mk 8

Type: All-weather fighter
Engines: Two 11,000lb (4,990kg) thrust Armstrong Siddeley Sapphire turbojets
Length: 56ft 3in (17.15m)
Wing span: 52ft 10in (16.10m) or Mach 0.95 maximum
Range: 1,500 miles (2,400km) with external fuel tanks
Armament: Four De Havilland Firestreak infra-red homing missiles, plus four 30mm Aden cannon
Crew: Pilot and navigator

Germany and regularly saw Russian MiG aircraft patrolling our joint border with East Germany. In November 1961 we all went to Malta for a few weeks, returning to Wattisham for Christmas, and in April 1962 it was back to RAF Gütersloh in Germany. By September 1962 we had a formation of five Javelins performing modest aerobatics—but the displays did not last long as the weather deteriorated!

'During my period on 41 we flew mostly high level—40,000 feet or so—with some low level 500 feet and some air firing at medium level. We were quite busy since we had a crew in an aircraft on standby at the end of the runway for most of this period during the night times.'

By the end of 1963, the Lightning-equipped fighter squadrons made the Javelin somewhat redundant and the need for a dedicated night

Above left: Members of No 41 Squadron pose in front of one of their aircraft, with a Firestreak missile displayed at the front, 1961. The OC, Wing Commander J. F. Pinnington, is seated centre.

Below: A Javelin Mk 8 of No 41 squadron dispatched to air show duties. The two bulges under the fuselage were external fuel tanks: like other RAF interceptors of the day, the Javelin was somewhat 'short-legged'.

RICHARD L. WARD

COURTESY PHILIP JARRETT

Top: The Squadron also operated a number of Javelin T. Mk 3 trainers, amongst the distinguishing features of which was the camouflaged (non-radar-carrying) nose and the revised cockpit canopy.

Above: A profile depicting a Javelin Mk 8 of the Squadron. The positioning of the serial number on the intake, and of the roundel forward of the intake, was encouraged by the fact that the big delta wing offered little space at the rear of the fuselage.

fighter was receding. So it was that 41 Squadron disbanded and lost its aircraft. It was later re-formed as a surface-to-air missile unit and in due course would fly manned aircraft again in the shape of Phantoms and, later, Jaguars at nearby RAF Coltishall—making occasional flyovers of Wattisham's runway until these latter aircraft, too, were given up in 2006.

COURTESY WATTISHAM AIRFIELD MUSEUM

Right: A scene from the Squadron's disbandment ceremony at Wattisham in 1963: AOCinC Air Marshal Sir Douglas Morris inspects; with him are Wing Commander Pinnington and the Station Commander, Group Captain Gibbs.

WATCHING EYES

B Y the north-west perimeter of the airfield, close to the Wattisham–Battisford road by Crash Gate 3, there remain disused dispersal loops from wartime days. In the late 1950s these were brought into use once again, to house radar systems of various types. The first occupants, in 1958, were a detachment from the USAFE who, under the name 'Anglia Control', managed the movements of the aircraft associated with US bases in East Anglia—Alconbury, Bentwaters, Chelveston, Lakenheath, Mildenhall, Wethersfield, Woodbridge and Sculthorpe. The unit had no connection with Wattisham, liaising with the RAF controllers at Neatishead and Bawdsey. One must assume that it was the site's altitude above sea level (Wattisham being one of the highest points in Suffolk) that caused it to be built so close the Station. RAF movements were, at the time, controlled by a similar site at Watton, which handled both military and civil aircraft movements.

USAFE personnel of the 1261st (and later the 2161st) Communications Squadron were housed here, control at the twin bases of Bentwaters and

Above: The main radar array at Anglia Control site, *circa* 1963. The brick structure on the right was the control centre proper.

Below: The abandoned site guardroom as it is today.

Left: The site in its heyday. The notice near the entrance reads 'United States Air Force Anglia Air Traffic Control Center'.

Below: Forty-five years on.

PAUL C. LOW, COURTESY LINN BARRINGER

AD HOC PUBLICATIONS

No 56 (F) Squadron

Motto
Quid si Cœlum Ruat
('What if heaven falls?')

Equipment
Hawker Hunter F. Mk 6 (1960–1961), English Electric Lightning F. Mk 1a (1961– 1965), F. Mk 3 (1965–1974), F Mk 6 (1974)

Above right: The early 1960s were indeed flamboyant times at Wattisham. Here No 56's Lightning F.1as and (lower photograph) a T.4 trainer brighten up a damp day on the flight line.

Below: A 'Firebirds' Lightning F.1a in profile.

Bottom: Joined by aircraft from Nos 19 and 92 Squadrons from RAF Leconfield, the Wattisham Lightnings prepare for a flypast over London in honour of the birth of Prince Edward, 10 March 1964.

square-topped fin and less obviously by the absence of any cannon armament; Red Top missiles gradually replaced the older Firestreaks. The cannon, erroneously deemed superfluous, were reinstated in the ultimate version of the aircraft, the Mk 6.

The year 1967 saw the transfer of No 56 Squadron to the sunny climes of Cyprus and the task of defending that island, but not before the formation of a small cadre of older Lightning Mk 1s and 1as as a Target Facilities Flight (TFF), aimed at giving the squadron pilots supersonic target training. These jets became very well known as the unit also adopted the solo aerobatic rôle for the RAF, with

Leading the Firebirds

Group Captain David Seward, Officer Commanding, No 56 (F) Squadron

I arrived at Wattisham as a Squadron Leader to take command of No 56 Squadron from Squadron Leader J. R. Rodgers in December 1961. At the time the Station was commanded by Group Captain Peter Horsley, soon to be succeeded by Group Captain David Simmons. OC Flying was Wing Commander Bill Howard, OC Engineering Wing was Wing Commander John Jenkins and OC Admin Wing was Wing Commander Percy Oldroyd. There were three flying squadrons at Wattisham—No 41 , commanded by Wing Commander John Pinnington flying Javelin Mk 8s; No 56; and No 111, commanded by Squadron Leader Dickie Wirdnam.

In February 1962 we detached four Lightnings to RAF Gütersloh in Germany to support and escort transport aircraft flying along the Berlin corridors. Soviet fighters had been harassing NATO transports using the corridors, and we were to provide fighter escorts and protection if required. The detachment lasted about two weeks, but we were not called to fly any escort sorties.

It had been decided by high command some months earlier that No 56 Squadron would be tasked with developing air-to-air refuelling (AAR) techniques for the Lightning using the Valiant tankers, and to produce Standard Operating Procedures (SOPs) for the overseas deployment of Lightning squadrons. The projected programme was to work up, initially, six pilots in the AAR role and to deploy two aircraft to Cyprus in July 1962. If that was successful, we were to work up the rest of the pilots in AAR and deploy the whole squadron to Cyprus in October. After initial briefings and the selection of the first six pilots, we hit a snag. During the previous twelve months or so we had been experiencing fire indications within the reheat area of the engines whilst not having reheat selected; we had lost, I think, two aircraft that had caught fire. The cause was traced to chafing of the hydraulic control pipes which moved as control inputs were applied, and the escaping fluid was seeping along the inside of the fuselage and igniting as it swirled in the jet efflux. It was therefore decided that all Mk 1 and 1a Lightnings would be re-piped. This was not expected to be a time-consuming modification, and in view of the AAR task No 56 Squadron's aircraft would be the first to be tackled. Alas, it took much longer: by the end of April we still had no modified aircraft.

We had a good social relationship with the 55th Tactical Fighter Squadron at Wethersfield, and at a joint 'Happy Hour' in April I mentioned to the 55th's CO that the F-100's and the Lightning's probe systems, apart for being on opposite wings, were virtually the same and that it might be a good idea if we had some AAR training in the F-100F. I put this suggestion to Fighter Command, and the situation must have been desperate because in less than a week we had agreement from both Fighter Command and HQ USAFE for the six pilots to receive six hours' tanking training in the Super Sabre using the KB-50 tanker. This we did, and it was very successful.

We started tanking with the Lightnings on 13 June with the Valiants, first 'dry' probing and then 'wet' (i.e., actually taking on fuel), using the same techniques as we had practised with the Americans. When we were efficient,

we flew a navigation sortie around the whole of the British Isles., and then another sortie twice around, simulating the flight to Cyprus. Apart from our radar, and TACAN, we had no navigation aids with which to rendezvous with the tankers, so we went, accompanied, in formation, the Valiant providing the navigation and fuel as required.

The deployment of the first two aircraft was very successful; we flew out on 23 July and returned three days later. To ensure that the maximum number of pilots received actual route experience, two different pilots flew the return trip, and once home we settled down to convert the entire squadron to AAR. When the time came for the full squadron deployment there were insufficient tankers available to see us to Cyprus. The main problem was the single-point drogue of the Valiant, plus the need always to have an

DAVID SEWARD

accompanying spare tanker to cover drogue failures. Thus, with the other operational tasks put upon the tanker force, there were simply not enough Valiants to go round. In the event we could only take four Lightnings on the second deployment, but, again, I had four pilots fly the outbound sortie and four different ones fly the return trip. I thus had twelve pilots route qualified.

We had proved that AAR with the Lightning could be achieved easily by the average pilot and that the aircraft was suitable for the task; moreover, although a full squadron deployment had not been demonstrated, we could see no insurmountable difficulties. In fact, twelve months would pass before the full squadron deployed to Cyprus, and this was accomplished in three waves of four Lightnings over a two-day period. Meanwhile we settled down to normal squadron duties, including intercept training, Quick Reaction Alert (QRA)—with two aircraft on armed standby at two minutes' readiness to investigate any unidentified aircraft entering our area of responsibility—and AAR training.

During late October we began to hear rumours that we were to be the next RAF Formation Aerobatic Team, and this was confirmed in November.

COURTESY DAVID SEWARD

Above: Firebirds over Suffolk. No 56 (F) would be the last RAF front-line squadron to form the official Aerobatic Team: henceforth the responsibilities would pass to the Central Flying School and training aircraft.

Left: Their flying helmets suitably embellished, and with neckwear to match, members of the 'Firebirds' team return from a training sortie.

We received very broad guidance. The main display for 1963 would be the Paris Air Show in June, and the routine was to based on a nine-ship formation which then split into two separate elements so as not to leave gaps in the performance. We reckoned that we should, in fact, have ten aircraft take off, with nine making up the main formation and the tenth man holding behind the spectators so that, when we split into two formations via a level 'break', he would join the rear formation and provide co-ordinated aerobatics with two flights of five aircraft. There were still gaps, so we introduced a solo man to carry out aerobatics when we were forming up or re-forming after a bomb-burst. We also had an airborne spare to fill in if we had any unserviceability. This plan required the use of twelve pilots, and we had fifteen to choose from. Allowing for sickness, leave and people away on courses etc., this meant that all the pilots on the Squadron were involved

In choosing the leaders I went purely on seniority. As Squadron Commander I was the formation leader, and my number two, who was also the deputy formation leader, was the 'B' Flight commander. He had been on No 74 Squadron during the previous year when they were the RAF team. The leader of the rear formation was the 'A' Flight commander, who had been on No 111 Squadron when they were the 'Black Arrows'. We reckoned we needed a name, so we called ourselves the 'Firebirds' because the Squadron badge depicted a phœnix rising from the ashes. (Actually we thought that it was a bird with its back end on fire—which pretty well summed up the Lightning in afterburner!) We painted our aircraft spines and tails red, and as this looked rather bland we also painted the leading edges of the wings and tail . We then devised a way of making smoke. We isolated the port flap fuel tank and led a pipe from there inside the strake which ran along the outside of the aircraft, feeding it back into the fuselage and attaching a small spray nozzle above the lower engine. We connected a small pump to the device and wired it up to the redundant gun trigger and filled the tank with diesel fuel. When we pressed the trigger, diesel was sprayed into the jet efflux and we got instant smoke.

So we had a name, coloured aircraft and smoke, and we worked the leaders up on solo aerobatics before starting the pilots flying in pairs doing steep turns, wing-overs and barrel rolls, working them in various positions until we were able to put them on the left or right wing positions. We then progressed to threes, fours and fives doing wing-overs, loops and rolls and formation changes during the manœuvres, and then formed the Big Nine.

Although the pilot training went well, we did hit some snags. The solo aeros man was promoted and posted just as we were getting started, and as we could not spare anyone to train up in time we managed to have No 111 Squadron's solo man detached to us for the duration. Then we experienced a mid-air collision in which one aircraft was lost and its pilot severely injured. The accident occurred during a 'bomb burst' in which the aircraft were supposed to fan out, but the No 2 tucked himself close to the

Above: Squadron Leader Dave Seward discusses tactics with the team.
Right: The team pose for the camera outside No 56 (F) Squadron headquarters at Wattisham.

Above: Diamond Nine, top of the loop and making smoke.

outside man and when they rolled out they touched and he had to eject. He never flew again, although the other pilot was able to land normally and the aircraft was serviceable the next day. We were given a replacement pilot who had been on No 92 Squadron's 'Blue Diamonds' team. Another problem appeared just after we started to work up the Big Nine formation: the aircraft's fin tips (which held the UHF antennas) started to work loose. The formation position was stepped down, but cine film showed clearly that the fins were never in the jet efflux. My aircraft was one of the first to have its fin tip work loose. It had always been the lead ship, but by coincidence it was also the aircraft that had made the most AAR contacts, and when refuelling it was common practice to fly into the drogue with the fin just burbling in the Valiant's jet efflux (thereby ensuring that the vertical position was correct). I pointed this out to Fighter Command, but they were adamant: 'No aerobatics in the nine formation!' Thereafter we could only do turns and formation changes before splitting into the two fives.

Our first public show was at Waterbeach in May and the second was North Weald in June. We then led the Queen's Birthday Flypast, after which we performed at the Paris Air Show on 13 and 16 June and received a standing ovation! During July and August we returned to normal training and then worked up again for the Battle of Britain displays in September. Our last two shows were at Wethersfield and for the Royal Observer Corps on 15 September. We then de-modified our aircraft, removed the smoke system and disbanded as the official RAF Formation Aerobatic Team.

I handed No 56 Squadron over to Squadron Leader I. R .Martin in October, having had a most stimulating tour. Wattisham was a very happy station. There was always a friendly rivalry between the squadrons, and I think we did a good and worthwhile job. I left to help form the new Lightning OCU at RAF Middleton St George, and then at RAF Coltishall, where in 1972 I became the Chief Instructor—but that's another story . . . .

pilots such as Bob Lightfoot and Russ Pengelly to be seen around the air-show circuit. The Flight's Lightning's adopted cat-like names such as 'Korky', 'Jinx' and 'Felix', while sporting an unofficial tail-fin badge based on the rear-view of a cat and its similarity to the rear-view of a Lightning—that being the only view seen of a TFF Lightning by trainee pilots.

It was at this time that, once more, No 111 Squadron were tasked with providing a formation display team. Under the leadership of Squadron Leader George Black, the team consisted of a nine-ship formation to

Top: A Target Facilities Flight Lightning Mk 1 at Wattisham.

Above: The revised paint scheme for No 56 Squadron's Lightning F.3s.

Below: Two-seat trainers facilitated type conversion and refresher flying. This T. Mk 5 is in 'Treble-One' markings, 1967.

McDONNELL DOUGLAS PHANTOM F.G.R. Mk 2

Type: Interceptor fighter
Engines: Two 20,500lb
(9,300kg) thrust Rolls-Royce
Spey 202 turbofans
Length: 56ft 3in (17.15m)
Wing span: 38ft 5in (11.71m)
Speed: Mach 1.9 maximum
Range: 1,200 miles (1,930km)
Armament: Four AIM-7
Sparrow and four AIM-9
Sidewinder air-to-air missiles,
plus other external ordnance
Crew: Pilot and navigator

AUTHOR

Above right: A Phantom F.G.R.
Mk 2 of No 56 Squadron at
Wattisham.

Below: Profile of a No 23
Squadron Phantom
F.G.R.2.

JOOP DE GROOT

receiver (RWR) fitting on the fin, and the aircraft were slowly upgraded accordingly.

Once No 56 Squadron had also re-equipped with Phantoms, Wattisham settled into the routine of deployments, exercises and QRA that was the lot of a fighter base in the late 1970s and 1980s. When received on to the squadrons, the aircraft were painted in the standard grey and green camouflage. Squadron markings had altered subtly as the years went by, but it fell to No 56 to come up with a colour scheme more suitable for air defence work. Similar trials were taking place in other air forces, with variations on light blue and grey the subject of the experimentation. In October 1978, XV474, coded 'F' with No 56 Squadron, was the first RAF aircraft to have what became known as the air-superiority scheme. Light grey overall with miniature roundels and squadron emblems was tried before a final scheme was settled on that used a pale colour for the emblems as well. However, *esprit de corps* meant that within a short while the emblems were back to their normal size and colour!

A minor diversion was provided in 1979, when, to commemorate the sixtieth anniversary of the first transatlantic crossing by Alcock and Brown, two aircraft from No 56

Sky Flash at Mach 1.6

Wing Commander Willem Felger, navigator, No 23 (F) Squadron

In the summer of 1980 No 23 Squadron was selected to conduct live firing trials to validate the high-level performance of the Sky Flash missile. The trial parameters were studied by our senior QWI (Qualified Weapons Instructor), Squadron Leader Kevin Mace, and crews were selected. Rehearsals of the profiles in the simulator showed that this was not going to be an easy task, but after a lot of practice we were fairly confident of doing the job. Rather than flying from Wattisham the trials were to be flown from STCAAME (Strike Command Air-to-Air Missile Establishment) at Valley because of the monitoring and preparation facilities and expertise there, and the missiles would be 'tweaked' by the relevant specialists. Because of the high speeds and altitudes required, the Phantoms had to be flown 'clean wing', that is, without external fuel tanks and other extraneous 'junk'. We loved flying like this because the aircraft went like stink and also because sorties were relatively short. The targets would be Stiletto, a small, rocket-propelled, supersonic missile launched from a Canberra. Although the Stiletto was very small, we were assured that it included reflectors that would make it easy to see it on radar and that its rocket motor left a distinctive vapour trail which we couldn't fail to spot. Oh yes—and Stilettos were hugely expensive, so it would be appreciated if we didn't screw up!

The speeds involved by both the fighters and the targets meant that a lot of room was needed to set up the profiles, which in turn meant the Hebrides range. This was quite a hike from Valley, and so we would be supported by Victor tankers to make up for our lack of range and also because we were going to be using rather a lot of reheat. Sadly the tankers would operate out of their home base at Marham rather than joining us at Valley (which would undoubtedly have added to the fun).

From day one the weather was the very dankest that Wales could throw at us. We flew in threes—a primary and a secondary firer and a photo-chase. The chase would use his gun sight to aim a camera and track the firer, and then switch to the missile from launch to impact. It sounded simple enough. The firer came off the tanker, accelerated down range to Mach 1.6 plus and zoomed up to where the sky was a beautiful royal blue. Meanwhile the Stiletto was going rather faster and higher than that, coming the other way, so things happened fast. For reasons of safety and telemetry the impact area was quite a small box, which had been confirmed as being free from ships

and other aircraft. The same system that gave us the rotten weather also provided a stonking crosswind, which made the offset quite sizeable, even at those speeds. Once the target was seen or radar, manœuvres to adjust the geometry for firing had to be bold and quick. The practice profiles had already shown that the photo-chase had a very challenging job, so a dedicated crew, Flight Lieutenants Al Cameron and Bill Medland, flew on every launch.

I flew with Major Jack Webb, our USAF exchange officer. We took off in thick cloud and poor visibility and set off for the tanker RV north of Benbecula. Still in cloud at 30,000 feet with the chase in close formation, we found the tanker, filled up with fuel and set off for the range. As we climbed higher, we flew into clear air and looked forward to having the vapour trial to help us.

There was no positive contact yet with the Canberra or the Stiletto, but we were off down-range like a scalded cat and were quickly above Mach 1.6 with Al tucked in behind. We got the Stiletto, came hard left and locked the radar. It doesn't like it, so switch to pulse mode and it settles. Reverse the turn, master arm 'live', camera on, and transmit the radio call—'Firing, firing . . . now!' A reassuring *bleep* from the trigger press, and a gentle *swoosh* as the missile leaves our jet aircraft. We see Al switch his attention from us to the missile's smoke . . . but where is the vapour trail from the target? As I count down the estimated time to impact there is a spectacular orange fireball (which we were not expecting) as Sky Flash and Stiletto hit each other at a huge combined speed. Meanwhile Al and Bill, who are still doing Mach 1.6 plus, are concentrating rather hard on avoiding the wreckage.

Speed and heart rate back under control, master arm to 'safe', camera off, fuel still okay—but where's the tanker? Answer: waiting patiently down in the murk north of Benbecula!

So it went on for three weeks. The good bits? Lots of missiles fired, some less successful than others, and some head-scratching by technicians to overcome the inevitable snags. The friendly hospitality of everyone at RAF Valley and the locals was terrific. The bad bits? The awful weather, tricky flying . . . and no, we never did see a single vapour trail from the Stiletto target!

Left: A Phantom F.G.R.2 of No 56 Squadron in the new colours taxies back to its HAS complex. One of these protective buildings can be seen in the background, and an aerial view of No 74's complex is featured on the title page of this book.

Right: Back home, the crew disembark preparatory to their debrief at Squadron head-quarters. Alongside the cockpit, the inflight refuelling probe is extended.

AD HOC PUBLICATIONS

Right: A flight of five Phantoms, tailhooks down, overflies Wattisham.

Far right: 'Sierra' of No 23 Squadron on the pan in 1982. The days of disruptive camouflage were now numbered.

AUTHOR

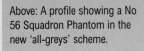

Above: A profile showing a No 56 Squadron Phantom in the new 'all-greys' scheme.

Right: Its braking parachute streaming, one of the Alcock and Brown commemorative aircraft lands on the main runway.

AUTHOR

AD HOC PUBLICATIONS

Squadron were painted in special colours and flown across the Atlantic by Flight Lieutenant Alcock (a grandson of the original) and Flight Lieutenant Browne (no relation). The aircraft were also unusual in bearing no serial markings, but they were in fact XV424 and XV486.

It was at about this time that a new programme was introduced, to help protect the RAF's valuable assets in the event of a sudden enemy bombing strike—the erection of hardened aircraft shelters (HAS), which began to appear at many front-line RAF stations. The construction of these had not yet started, however, when it fell once again to 'Foxtrot' from No 56 Squadron to try out an emergency landing system for Wattisham. The short cross-runway was in poor state of repair, and would certainly have given a 30-ton-plus Phantom a problem or two if forced to land there. So, early one winter's morning the minor road passing the base was closed to traffic while an intrepid aircrew carried out 'touch-and-go's' on the perimeter track near the lane. Although no mishaps occurred, the building of shelters, and the subsequent use of this track for taxying aircraft to the runway, probably precluded any further development. With the building of the HASs at the western end of the airfield, Hangar 3 became empty and life changed dramatically for No 56

Tiger Trails

Group Captain Dick Northcote OBE BA, *Officer Commanding, No 74 (F) Squadron*

In July 1984 I and a team of aircrew arrived at the Marine Fighter Attack Training Squadron (VMFAT) to fly ten familiarisation sorties on the Phantom F-4S, a model was very similar to the F-4J which No 74 (F) Squadron was about to take on the air defence rôle at RAF Wattisham. The acquisition of the aircraft was a 'quick fix' to replace the F.G.R.2s that had been sent to the Falkland Islands. Prior to this, fifteen F-4Js were being completely gutted and refurbished at North Island San Diego. The plan was to send teams of aircrew from No 74 (F) to the US to fly the aircraft back from San Diego in groups of three as they completed their refurbishment. The exercise was known as 'Tiger Trail' and numbered from 1 to 5.

Following some familiarisation sorties at MCAS Yuma, we transferred to North Island, flew three or four test flights on the three aircraft that were ready and then flew the aircraft home during the period 27–30 August 1984. The flight back to Britain was certainly different. We returned via Wright Patterson AFB and Goose Bay. At Wright Patterson one of our drop tanks was severely damaged by a flailing Houchin starter hose and threatened to delay the trip by several days until our enterprising ground crew borrowed one from the local F-4 unit on the base and replaced the damaged one. (I don't think we ever paid for it!)

The flight into Goose Bay in the dark across hundreds of miles of unpopulated frozen wasteland certainly got my attention. We could not be issued with proper 'goony' survival suits for sub-zero temperatures as they were not compatible with the version of F-4J we had taken over. As we flew for several hours at around 1,000 feet in complete darkness across the ice, I couldn't help but hope that the 'Js' had been properly refurbished! They had been, and we landed safely at around bar-opening time. We had a day to wait before flying back to Wattisham, and by chance the Base Commander was an old friend of mine from Staff College days. He challenged my team to a Canadian Air Force *vs* Royal Air Force games night in the mess that night (but I have no idea who won!).

A few months later, on 11–13 December, I carried out the final 'Tiger Trail 5' with the last three aircraft and so No 74 (F) Squadron became fully equipped at Wattisham with fifteen F-4Js. On this last trail, Group Captain Tony Park, OC RAF Wattisham, flew the No 2 aircraft. We still had not resolved the survival suit problem, and as we flew out of Goose Bay on the final leg we could not help but notice the enormous icebergs below us stretching as far as the eye could see. Survival in that sea would have been a bit of a problem!

I was OC the Squadron from that period until 7 November 1986. Our sister squadron was No 56 (F), run by Wing Commander Ali McKay. Initially the Squadrons were based in the old hangar units while the new shelters were being built, but we moved across to the new units in the middle of 1985.

The base was an extremely active one during my two and a half years there. We were tasked with all the normal activities of a fighter base—from operational Tactical Evaluations starting in the middle of the night that would last several days and involve the entire base, including families, to week-end parties that could also last several days! We spent several weeks a year away from the base at Annual Practice Camps for air-to-air gunnery and so on. The chaps on the Squadron had their own version of TACEVAL: half a dozen or so would turn up on my doorstep with clipboards in hand to give marks out of ten for such things as 'speed of delivering the first drink', 'amount of drink supplied', 'quality of 'eggybakes' (egg and bacon sandwiches) etc. Not a big problem—except that the evaluation normally started after they had been thrown out of the last pub!

I am pleased to say that there were no serious flying accidents on No 74 Squadron during this period, probably because most of the aircrew and groundcrew were very experienced from the start. We had had, after all, to become operational as quickly as possible!

Below: A test flight for the 'Tigers' over the Californian coast. The refurbished aircraft were flown to Wattisham in batches of three.

McDONNELL DOUGLAS F-4J (UK) PHANTOM

Type: Interceptor fighter
Engines: Two 17,900lb (8,120kg) thrust General Electric J79-GE-10B turbojets
Length: 58ft 4in (17.78m)
Wing span: 38ft 5in (11.71m)
Speed: Mach 2.4 maximum
Range: 2,000 miles (3,200km) with external fuel
Armament: Four AIM-7 Sparrow and four AIM-9 Sidewinder air-to-air missiles, plus other external ordnance
Crew: Pilot and navigator

YOUR Tigers are coming

Below: 'G-for-George' under a threatening sky, safely home on the 'pan'. The paintwork that had been applied to the new arrivals, dubbed 'duck egg green' by some, caused a stir as it was quite different from that of the rest of the RAF's Phantom fleet.

Squadron. With unit headquarters, operations HQ and dedicated planning facilities, plus the facilities to 'garage' all their aircraft at this complex, the old adage that 'if there are aircraft on the pan, they are flying' no longer worked.

In 1982, Britain found itself in challenging position of having to defend its people at the opposite end of the Atlantic, in the Falkland Islands, and the events 7,000 miles away were to have an important effect on Wattisham during 1983 and 1984. Once the conflict in the South Atlantic was over, it was obvious that a fighter defence system for the islands would be vital in case the Argentinians ever felt like chancing their arm a second time. Thus the decision was taken to station the Wattisham-based No 23 Squadron at the airfield at Port Stanley, relieving No 29 Squadron, which had been sent there immediately after the re-occupation.

Once No 23 Squadron had been established on the islands, thoughts returned to air defence at home and of how to deal with the fact that the Royal Air Force was now, in effect, a Phantom squadron short. The solution to this quandary lay in one of the strangest, albeit most successful, decisions that the British Government had taken in many years: it decided to purchase a complete squadron of fifteen second-hand F-4J Phantoms surplus to US Navy requirements and languishing in the desert in Arizona. The F-4J was chosen as it was the nearest in terms of specifications to the F-4K currently equipping two fighter squadrons in the RAF, although after going through the reclamation programme in the United States the resulting aircraft were almost to F-4S standard.

Thus, at sunset on 30 August 1984, with two jets from No 56 Squadron escorting them for the last section of their journey, three F-4J Phantoms of the newly re-formed No 74 Squadron arrived at Wattisham's threshold. Over the next few weeks the remainder of the refurbished Phantoms arrived, to be housed in the southern HAS site. Various shades of colour were noted, but another big shock came when a black-finned F-4J arrived.

AD HOC PUBLICATIONS

No 74 (F) Squadron

Motto
I Fear No Man

Equipment
McDonnell Douglas F-4J (UK)
Phantom

Ostentatious unit markings had been rather frowned upon by higher authority since the days of the Lightning, and it was deemed only a matter of time before the black was removed. Far from it! Slowly all the aircraft appeared with black tailfins, which set the Squadron's insignia off so well. Once one unit does something like this (and gets away with it), others can be relied upon to follow: most of the home-based and RAF Germany squadrons eventually took up the theme, and it was only a matter of time before No 56 Squadron revisited the old 'Firebirds' scheme from the 1960s by having the tailfins of its aircraft painted red and adorned with the phœnix.

Although it took some time to be cleared for operations, the F-4J was a hugely popular aircraft amongst its aircrews. With a better search and attack radar, and with less power but a faster response from the American J79 engines than the Speys in the F-4M, the F-4J was not as quick at low

Above left: Armed with live missiles, a No 74 Squadron Phantom on 'Q' at Wattisham.

Below: Profile depicting a No 74 Squadron F-4J (UK) with a full war load.

Bottom: The return of colour: a No 56 Squadron F.G.R.2 in its final paint scheme.

Opposite: Wattisham's 'Q' shed, with two 'Tigers' on alert.

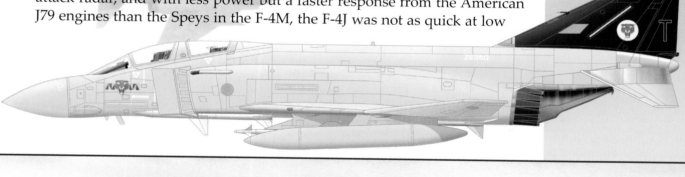

AUTHOR

'Q'

Wing Commander Dave Gledhill, navigator, No 56 (F) Squadron

The high-pitched 'alert' klaxon pierced the night air. Instantly awake, I hit the light switch and threw the hairy Air Force-issue blankets on to the floor. Disentangling myself from the sheets which had wrapped themselves around me like an eel, I groped at the side of the bed for my immersion suit, which I had carefully laid at the side of the bed before going to sleep. I slid my feet into the rubberised socks. Pulling the heavy material up and over my torso, I struggled into the heavy suit. The rubber of the neck seal felt cold and unforgiving as it tore at my hair before popping tightly around my neck. A quick drag on the heavy zip which cut diagonally across my chest, and I was stepping into my flying boots and stumbling out of the door towards the hangar.

The Quick Reaction Alert sheds at RAF Wattisham lay at the easterly end of the airfield just a short distance from the relatively short, 7,500-foot runway. For most of the year, two Phantom air defence fighters sat on alert twenty-four hours a day, seven days a week; the only respite was when the duty passed over to the other southern base at RAF Coningsby in Lincolnshire. The metal sheds, painted in a sickly shade of green and slashed by the random zig-zag camouflage pattern, made a poor effort to blend in with the surrounding countryside. The sheds housed the two adjacent bays for the alert fighters, a small brick-built annex providing daytime shelter for the aircrew and groundcrew who made up the QRA team. At this early hour, only the harsh yellow of the sodium lights that ringed the facility cut the darkness of the surrounding airfield; the barbed wire of the security fence was the only clear sign of the importance of this unassuming collection of buildings. Alongside the complex, two ancient runway caravans, rescued from the days when the Vulcan bomber had held nuclear alert, had been 'plumbed in' to provide sleeping accommodation for crews who were confined to this austere facility during their regular 24-hour sentence. As the siren sounded, the groundcrew began spilling from the first caravan and the doors of the hangars slid noisily back to reveal the squat and functional profile of the Phantom fighter jets. As the doors clanged to a stop, the sodium light reflected menacingly on the Sidewinder infra-red missiles mounted on the wing pylons but still shrouded by their protective 'Noddy caps'.

As I rounded the open door, there was a frantic scene of activity. To an outsider it would appear as little short of panic; to the players it was a well-drilled routine, each of us having a precise rôle to fill. We were on 'Readiness 10', which meant that this aircraft had to be airborne within ten minutes of a scramble message, wheels in the well and ready to intercept any intruder who strayed into UK airspace. Rushing to the base of the ladder, I stepped into the torso harness which held my survival gear and pulled the bulky green lifejacket over my shoulders. A quick click on the breastplate and the jacket was fastened, and I wriggled to tighten the straps around my groin

and across my chest. This harness would act as my parachute if I was forced to eject, and it was to my eternal benefit to ensure that it fitted snugly. Up the ladder dragging on my bone dome, I stepped over the edge of the cockpit on to the Martin Baker ejection seat and dropped into the hard pad which was to be my 'armchair' for the next seven hours. Swiftly plugging the PEC into the housing on my left, I connected the intercom lead and I hit the floor-mounted transmit switch with my right foot. As I began strapping into my ejection seat, the face of the 'liney' appeared on the ladder to assist with my top straps. It seemed like an hour since the intrusive hooter had broken our slumber, but in reality it had been only two minutes. As I glanced ahead, I could see the warm air of the hangar spilling out into the cold night air.

'Wing Ops, 71 standing by.' There would be no delay.

'71, vector 010, climb Angels 250, contact Neatishead Fighter Stud 74, scramble, scramble, scramble! Acknowledge.'

'71 scrambling.'

'On in the front,' I heard as Guy, my pilot, checked in on intercom, his exertion obvious as he was panting slightly. The engines were already spooling up.

'I've got the scramble message.' In response, the engines rose in pitch.

'In Nav, clear to go.'

The slowest part of the whole scramble procedure was waiting for the inertial navigation system to align. Even a rapid alignment took ninety seconds, and the wait for the instrument to complete its sequence seemed interminable.

'In Nav, clear to go,' I repeated above the racket of the engines. Below us, there was a flurry of activity as one 'liney' disappeared below the aircraft to remove the chocks and disconnect the external power set. The Crew Chief was already running out into the darkness to marshal us out of the hangar.

'72's on,' I heard from the other aircraft. Fantastic! The Boss had taken a full minute extra to get out of his 'pit'. That would make up for the chewing off I'd received for being late for briefing last week.

We surged forward. We would launch as a singleton but '72' would remain on readiness, engines running until we were safely airborne and had completed our weapons checks and reported serviceable. The jet lumbered across the taxiway, sluggish on the ground, and on to the fast access which joined the runway 1,000 feet in from the threshold. The runway length at Wattisham was about the shortest strip the F-4 Phantom could live with. This bird was fitted with a full missile load of four Sparrows and four Sidewinders as well as a heavy centreline fuel tank in addition to the normal underwing tanks. With a cold jet woken from its slumber we could afford no problems. Ahead, the blue edge lights and the centreline greens of the taxiway glowed brightly as we eased towards the runway . . .

altitude but it was speedier at height. Once operational, No 74 (F) Squadron was tasked with flying the resurrected solo Phantom 'demo' at air shows, the slot having been abandoned a couple of years previously after the loss of the allocated aircraft in a crash at Abingdon.

In the late 1980s, events in the Eastern Bloc, long thought to be from where 'the threat' would come, were to have an effect on the Phantom that nobody had foreseen. The collapse of the Warsaw Pact and the resultant arms reduction treaties led to the Phantom being sacrificed. The original plans had been that the aircraft would continue in service until 2007, to be replaced (one assumes) by Typhoons, but suddenly the stationing of two fighter squadrons in RAF Germany and nine in Britain was no longer considered necessary.

As the aircraft were withdrawn and the squadrons disbanded, Wattisham found itself the home of a growing number of redundant Phantoms.

Above: Tigers close up and personal, here flying a Spey-engined Phantom following the phasing out of the F-4Js. The blue 'missile' under the aircraft's belly is a Sky Flash acquisition (practice) round. The pilot is sporting a natty line in headgear!

Right: Sad homecoming: surplus Phantoms left to their fate on Wattisham's scrapheap. These particular aircraft are finished in the markings of 'Treble-One'—the Squadron that for so many years had known Wattisham as its home before it was re-located to RAF Leuchars in Scotland.

The Final Option

The Author

The Bloodhound surface-to-air missile units in Germany were replaced in the early 1980s by mobile Rapier batteries, and the Bloodhounds were relocated in Britain. A Flight of No 25 Squadron was stationed at Wattisham in 1983, located at the north-eastern end of the airfield, by the old wartime bomb dump.

The Bloodhound was highly regarded throughout its career, thanks mainly to its constant updates. The associated Type 87 Scorpion radar unit was mounted on a steel tower, and most of this latter structure still stands on the airfield today.

Bloodhound was a 'final option': it was necessary in the event of attacking enemy aircraft managing to avoid the defending fighters, and it was able to hit targets flying at altitudes of up to 65,000 feet and at a maximum range of some 85 miles. The Flight continued in service until its disbandment with the standing down of all Bloodhounds in 1991.

JOHN A. SMITH

Above: A visit to RAF Wattisham by Queen Elizabeth II was a highlight of the 1980s. Here Her Majesty is inspecting one of No 74 Squadron's hardened aircraft shelters, 7 June 1985.

DICK NORTHCOTE

COURTESY GRAHAM CLARKE

Above right: As good a 'reach' as the Phantom had, its range could be further extended by the use of air-to-air refuelling (AAR).

The logic, therefore, of having a squadron of aircraft of different specification no longer held, and the F-4J was withdrawn after seven years of service and replaced with the F.G.R.2.

As a final gesture, nine Phantom F-4Js were launched one January morning in 1991 to fly a Diamond Nine over the locality before landing on Wattisham's zero-five runway. As if in salute, as each aircraft turned off the runway it folded its wings to taxi back to the HAS site, using the ex-Navy kit with which this one version was still fitted.

Reference has been made to the siting of No 74 Squadron's headquarters on the southern side of the airfield. This positioned the aircraft such that for access to or egress from the main runway (depending on

AUTHOR

89

Number One Hitter

Group Captain Graham Clarke, Officer Commanding, No 74 (F) Squadron

I had flown Phantom F.G.R.2s while on No 92 Squadron at Wildenrath in Germany, and so I was intrigued when the opportunity came along to fly with No 74 Squadron at Wattisham, How would the J79-engined F-4Js compare with the Spey-engined Phantoms with which I was familiar?

They proved to be rather different, and I have to say that, from a pilot's point of view, the ex-US Navy aircraft had some advantages. In fact, I and my colleagues on the Squadron liked it immensely. For one thing, the mere task of operating the throttles was easier: the 'British' Phantoms' throttles had no hydraulic assistance and it could be quite difficult to get them moving. The general 'feel' of the aircraft was very much lighter, too. This was especially evident when full afterburner was selected: the -J version was more akin to the Lightning in this respect. There were fewer limitations on what you could do once in the air, and these often showed themselves in subtle ways. For example, the re-engineering of the F.G.R.2 to accept the Rolls-Royce engines had produced a much thinner 'divide' between the paired tailpipes, the effect of which was to impose a greater 'g' imitation if an underbelly tank happened to be fitted.

There were drawbacks, of course, particularly on the engineering side. Although spares were plentiful (not least because, after the fall of the Shah of Persia, spare engines etc originally destined for Iran started to be come stockpiled in the US), they were expensive. The J79, moreover, had no integral starting facility, and so a heavy external Houchin was required for every flight. However, more positively, the J79 could be readily extracted from the Phantom airframe for major servicing; the Speys posed problems in this respect. We had the F-4S-standard digital radar in the F-4J—a further advantage—and, curiously, the greenish blue-grey of the aircraft's paintwork made it far less easy to spot visually in the air than a Spey-engined Phantom.

Remembrances? The honour of commanding the Squadron, of course; and, with Flight Lieutenant Sean O'Brien as WSO in ZE359, becoming the 'number one hitter' using the Gatling gun on a towed target during Armament Practice Camp in Cyprus. We in No 74 Squadron went over to the F.G.R.2s anyway, at the end, so for many the Phantom experience came full circle. On balance, these aircrews would rather have stayed with the F-4Js!

GRAHAM CLARKE

Right: A 'Tiger' banking over the Suffolk countryside. This aircraft and that depicted at the foot of the page are F.G.R.2s. One clue—the F-4Js never had the fin-top RWR fairing, their warning gear being mounted along the engine intakes.

GRAHAM CLARKE

Left: Wing Commander (as he then was) Graham Clarke—with Sean O'Brien in the back seat, at the controls of ZE359, with a Gatling gun pod under the aircraft's belly.

Below: Sleeping Tiger: 'G-for-George', now with a black tailfin, outside its HAS at the south-western end of Wattisham airfield.

AD HOC PUBLICATIONS

COURTESY GRAHAM CLARKE

Left: During an exercise off St Mawgan in June 1991, the radome on CO Graham Clarke's F.G.R.2 XT891, for no apparent reason, suffered delamination, with this result.

Bottom: No doubting the squadron to which this celebratory Phantom belongs. Just for fun—nothing serious.

COURTESY GRAHAM CLARKE

wind direction) the aircraft had to taxi past Crash Gate 2. Those readers familiar with Wattisham will know that this is the favourite position for all the local aviation enthusiasts, and, as a result, a considerable rapport built up between the aircrews and the public. Pilots and navigators (more correctly Weapons System Officers) were taxying past a mere fifty yards away from their adoring public, and a wave became the norm; if you were lucky, there was a pause long enough for photographs to be taken.

In 1992 the rôle of Phantom demonstrator was recreated for this final year, and, in a fly-off, Archie Liggatt (pilot) and Mark Mainwaring (WSO) were chosen to crew the aircraft. In what became generally accepted as one of the best RAF Phantom 'demos', this pair were to be seen at virtually all the major air shows across the country that year as well as a good few in Europe. It was during one such show, No 74's own 'Families Day', that, with no public access permitted and the roads and fields around Wattisham full of spectators, a panel came adrift from the aircraft in a wing-over performed safely outside the field. The display carried on with no realisation of what had happened, while the piece of panel dropped safely just inside the airfield!

With the announcement that the No 74 Squadron colours would be transferred to 4 Flying Training School at RAF Valley, equipped with Hawks, and that No 56 would hand its standard to the newly numbered Tornado F.3 Operational Conversion Unit at RAF Coningsby to became No 56 (Reserve) Squadron, the final days of the Phantom were fast approaching. The aircraft was laid to rest in 1992, and after a photo-call for the public and aviation enthusiasts, front-line RAF combat squadrons left Wattisham for the last time.

AUTHOR

HOVERING HEROES

AT a time when all links with the Royal Air Force were being broken, it came as something of a surprise when, in July 1994, Wattisham became the home of 'B' Flight of No 22 Squadron, with a complement of Sea Kings. With some irony, the barns that were once the home of air-defence fighters on alert were replaced with a large complex including hangar facilities to house two rescue helicopters on alert!

With a history reaching back to the days of World War I, No 22 Squadron has been tasked with air–sea rescue since February 1955, serving at Thorney Island, initially with Bristol Sycamores. Equipped later with Whirlwinds, Wessexes and finally Sea Kings, the Squadron has been based at St Mawgan and Finningley, with its three flights variously at Valley, Felixstowe, Tangmere, Martlesham Heath, Manston, Coltishall, Leuchars, Leconfield, Finningley, Chivenor, Brawdy and even Christmas Island. It arrived at Wattisham with some controversy, however, as it was felt that the new location, at the expense of two Wessex each at Coltishall and Manston, signalled a large loss of capacity and coverage.

Rescue services are co-ordinated by RAF Aeronautical Rescue Centre (ARCC) at Kinloss, although the Squadron is allowed to 'self-scramble' too. Tasking is almost exclusively for civilian purposes: modern safety systems in military aircraft and the consequential low level of aircraft losses mean that in many years since arriving at Wattisham, the number of military scrambles was less than five per cent of the total. The reasons for call-outs range from a lost Lilo from some beach, through major marine rescues to human organ collection and delivery.

A review of rescue services for the year 2006 showed an increase in 'scrambles' of some 25 per cent over the previous year, the vast majority being civilian emergencies; military rescues (the *raison d'être* of the Flight) were described as amounting to a mere handful. This very public task is carried out with a total manning of 18 aircrew and some 40 maintenance engineers, supported by a small operations staff.

No 22 Squadron
The *pi* symbol dates back to the time when, in World War I, the Squadron's aircraft habitually took off over the 7th Wing headquarters in France. The Maltese cross recalls deployments in that island

Motto
Preux et Audacieux
('Valiant and Brave')

Equipment
Westland Sea King
H.A.R. Mk 3A

Left: Off on another sortie. The area of operations for No 22 Squadron takes in the eastern English Channel and the southern North Sea, plus the whole of the south-east England land mass, from King's Lynn to Dover.

WESTLAND SEA KING H.A.R. Mk 3A

Type: Air–sea rescue helicopter
Engines: Two 1,500shp (1,120kW) thrust Rolls-Royce Gnome turboshafts
Fuselage length: 57ft 2in (17.42m)
Rotor diameter: 62ft 0in (18.90m)
Speed: 144mph (230kph)
Range: 750 miles (1,200km)
Armament: None
Crew: Pilot, co-pilot, navigator and winchman

AUTHOR

Right: One of No 22 Squadron's two Sea Kings—and a very welcome sight to many who have been in trouble.

Left: The Squadron insignia as carried on its bright yellow helicopters—twenty-two over seven equals *pi*.

Below: The Sea King Mk 3A's 'office'.

The Wattisham Flight is on fifteen minutes' readiness during the day and 45 minutes' at night, the unit being totally self-sufficient and having no link to the Wattisham Army facility. Maintenance is now contracted-out to civilian companies, and recent press (2006) has suggested that it is only a matter of time before the entire United Kingdom air–sea rescue service goes the same way. At present, however, the sight of a yellow Sea King can only bring the greatest feeling of relief to a downed airman, a sick seaman or that child with the misplaced Lilo.

Since the Sea Kings arrived, the trusty H.A.R.3s have been replaced with the new-build Mk 3A, which offers an automated hover system, enabling the aircraft to remain over a fixed point no matter what the conditions. One wag was heard to remark that it would be possible to set the machine in the hover, climb down the rope ladder, return to the mess for a cup of tea then after suitable relaxation climb back on board to resume the flight. Whether this has been tested in anger yet has to be established!

AD HOC PUBLICATIONS

Right: Ready for all emergencies —including those in the middle of the night.

AD HOC PUBLICATIONS

NEW TENANTS

AN announcement came in late 1991 that Wattisham was to become an Army Air Corps station, called Wattisham Airfield, and house a large consignment of helicopters. Building work took place at a phenomenal rate, new accommodation, three huge hangars, a new headquarters building between the old hangars 2 and 3 and the removal of the famous Q-sheds being the main visual changes. A twelve-foot-high chain-link fence was placed around the airfield.

Established on the airfield in the summer of 1993, the Army Air Corps' presence was brought about by the relocation from Germany of 3 and 4 Regiments, the caretakers of some forty Lynx A.H.7 and 9 helicopters and about twenty Gazelle A.H.1s. All came under the banner of the 24th Air-mobile Brigade, with its HQ at Colchester Garrison. Also in residence is 7 Battalion REME, the Army's second-line repair unit for all helicopters, and for which new facilities have been built on the old cross runway at the western end of the field.

Drastic changes took place on 1 September 1999 with the formation of a new unit within the Army's 4th Division to be known as 16th Air Brigade, consisting of the amalgamated brigades of 24 Airmobile and the 5th Airborne. With the TOW missile-equipped Lynx getting long in the tooth, the Brigade has finally been re-equipped with the Apache A.H.1, unarguably the best attack helicopter in the world. It has an armoured cockpit with multi-functional displays and the pilot (rear seat) and gunner are equipped with infra-red vision equipment to facilitate sighting

Above and below: The Apache A.H.1, its outline dominated by the immense Longbow radar above the rotor head. The swivelling Chain Gun is mounted beneath the cockpit, while stub wings permit the carriage of other ordnance.

GARY STEDMAN

94

Right: The Army Air Corps' equipment when it first moved into Wattisham included the Westland Lynx. This example carries United Nations identification markings for the Kosovo deployments of the 1990s.

Below: Like the Lynx, the Gazelle observation/reconnaissance helicopter is also being phased out of AAC service. The type is known to its crews affectionately as 'The Whistling Chicken Leg'.

at night. It also has Longbow radar, found above the rotor, further enhancing its target-acquisition system. As well its potent Hughes chain gun, the Apache can tote Hellfire missiles, rockets and extra fuel tanks on its sponsons.

Although the credit for the first Apache to arrive at Wattisham goes to a helicopter that 'went tech' and was obliged to divert during August 2000, it was January 2005 before the first operational pair arrived. Deliveries were delayed at first by a shortage of crews, but the numbers gradually increased and the Gazelles and Lynx A.H.9s (known colloquially as 'Wheelbarrows') slowly disappeared. The number of Lynx Mk 7s increased as uniformity was adopted across the squadrons. 662 and 663 Squadrons of 3 Regiment became the first Apache-equipped units,

WESTLAND APACHE A. H. Mk 1

Type: Attack helicopter
Engines: Two 2,240shp (1,670kW) thrust Rolls-Royce RTM 322 turboshafts
Length (rotors turning): 58ft 1in (17.70m)
Rotor diameter: 48ft 0in (14.63m)
Speed: 250mph (400kph)
Range: 1,100 miles (1,770km)
Armament: One M230 Chain Gun, plus Hellfire or Stinger missiles or CRV 7 rocket pods
Crew: Pilot and aircraft commander

although not before 663 Squadron had deployed to Iraq as part of Operation 'Telic' in 2003.

The year 2007 saw the Apache crews of 3 Regiment deployed to Afghanistan, replacing those of 9 Regiment who had been in the theatre for some time. The Apache units from Dishforth replaced 4 Regiment's Lynx and Gazelle units during the year and so, with the exception of those assigned to the training unit at Middle Wallop, all the Army Air Corps' Apaches are now based at Wattisham. With these changes in place, and with 7 Regiment REME now responsible for the maintenance of the entire Apache fleet, the future of Wattisham seems assured.

Since October 2000 the skies of Suffolk have been the beat of police helicopter G-SUFF, a very sophisticated Eurocopter EC.135. Equipped with today's best detection tools, this front-line aid for the Suffolk Constabulary has become a common sight in the Wattisham area. The helicopter was jointly funded by HM Government and Suffolk Police and was widely reported as costing a handsome £2 million. The support unit is based in the one of the old HAS complexes, occupying one of the shelters that for so long housed the mighty Phantoms of No 74 Squadron.

A Police Support Unit offers a scanning capability equivalent to many hundreds of police officers on the ground (and taking a fraction of the time) as well as a capability to pursue from the safety of the air; moreover, sophisticated surveillance equipment can be transported where needed fast and efficiently.

G-SUFF flies, on average, some 1,400 missions and more than 700 hours a year. Success rates are very high, figures for 2006 to the end of October, for example, showing some 30 missing persons located, 117 arrests made and the recovery of over £150,000 worth of stolen property. All this is carried out with a strength of seven officers under the supervision of one sergeant and three civilian aircrew.

The normal close liaison of the Suffolk ASU with that of Essex and Cambridgeshire will increase with the centralisation of helicopter servicing at Wattisham in the near future. The HAS will be equipped as a workshop and servicing of all three helicopters will be carried out by an Engineering Manager and two engineers.

Above: G-SUFF, the EC.135 operated by the Suffolk ASU, hovers close to the old blast pens near one of Wattisham's HAS complexes. Only four counties in the United Kingdom do not now have access to a designated Police Air Support Unit—a testimony to the efficiency of such a tool.

Below: A massive Ukrainian-registered Antonov An-124-100 comes into land at Wattisham, April 2008, bringing three AAC Apache helicopters back from live weapons training exercises in Arizona. How times have changed . . .

AUTHOR